WAYNE RICKERSON

THE WINNING HAND

Making the Most of Your Family's Personality Differences

NAVPRESS ®

A MINISTRY OF THE NAVIGATORS
P.O. BOX 6000, COLORADO SPRINGS, COLORADO 80934

The Navigators is an international Christian
organization. Jesus Christ gave His followers
the Great Commission to go and make disciples
(Matthew 28:19). The aim of The Navigators is to
help fulfill that commission by multiplying laborers
for Christ in every nation.

NavPress is the publishing ministry of The Navigators. NavPress publications are tools to help
Christians grow. Although publications alone cannot make disciples or change lives, they can help
believers learn biblical discipleship, and apply what
they learn to their lives and ministries.

Cover illustration: Mark Chickinelli

Unless otherwise identified, all Scripture in this
publication is from *The Living Bible* (TLB), © 1971,
owned by assignment by the Illinois Regional
Bank N.A. (as trustee), used by permission of
Tyndale House Publishers, Inc., Wheaton, IL
60189. Another version used is the *Holy Bible: New
International Version* (NIV). Copyright © 1973, 1978,
1984, International Bible Society. Used by permission of Zondervan Bible Publishers.

Printed in the United States of America

Contents

PART II. A Winning Hand in Parenting

PART III. Other Winning Hands

Author

Wayne Rickerson is the founder and director of People Dynamics, a counseling, resource-development, and seminar organization based in Phoenix, Arizona. *The Winning Hand* is his fifteenth book on marriage and family relationships.

Wayne graduated from Puget Sound Christian College and Golden Gate Baptist Theological Seminary. He is an ordained minister and has spent fifteen years as director of family ministries in churches. He is recognized as a pioneer in the development of family ministries in local churches during the mid 1970s. Wayne is an adjunct professor at Denver Conservative Baptist Seminary in the Doctor of Ministry program, Marriage and Family Counseling.

Wayne and his wife, Janet, have three daughters—Heidi, Liesl, and Bridget.

Introduction

Many families suffer painful conflict because they do not understand or accept this simple truth: *People are different.* The purpose of this book is to help you understand the strengths and weaknesses of your own personality and the personalities of others in your family, so that all family relationships can be improved.

Every attempt has been made to make this book as understandable and useful as possible. Features include:

- ♦ Personality inventories have been included for children, teens, and adults to help you discover the personality styles of each family member.
- ♦ A card theme. To help make the material easy to understand, remember, and apply, a playing card theme is used throughout the book.
- ♦ Play. This acronym will help you apply the material:

Promoting strengths
Limiting weaknesses
Accepting personality
Your compatibility

♦ Action plan sheets will help you immediately apply what you learn.

FOUR BASIC PERSONALITY STYLES

This book is based on the basic personality styles first observed centuries ago by such notables as Hippocrates and Aristotle. The original Greek terms for the four temperaments and the corresponding terms that will be used in this book are matched below. Note that the first letters spell out the word *CARD.*

Melancholic = Conscientious
Phlegmatic   = Amiable
Sanguine   = Relational
Choleric   = Dominant

The validity and usefulness of the basic Greek temperaments, or personality styles, have been well documented by such respected authorities as Dr. John Geier, Ph.D., professor of behavioral science and communication at the University of Minnesota. He developed the Personal Profile System now produced by Performax Systems International, Inc., which changes the four Greek terms to the acronym DISC: Dominant, Influencing, Steadiness, and Compliance.[1] Performax's DISC has been used extensively by many organizations and companies to increase communication and enhance team building.

David W. Merrill, author of *Personal Styles and Effective Performance,* uses yet another adaptation of the four Greek temperaments. These are Driver, Expressive, Amiable, and Analytical.[2]

The following chart compares the Greek terms to corresponding terms of Geier, Merrill, and the CARD personality style used in this book.

> GREEK (Hippocrates)—Melancholic, Phlegmatic, Sanguine, Choleric
> CARD PERSONALITY STYLES (Rickerson)—Conscientious, Amiable, Relational, Dominant
> DISC PERSONAL PROFILE (Geir-Performax)—Dominant, Influencing, Steadiness, Compliance
> PERSONAL STYLES (Merrill/Reid)—Analytical, Amiable, Expressive, Driver

Understanding personality styles plays an important part in completing the parenting puzzle. Personality styles, however, are not the final word on parenting. Applying all the material in this book perfectly would not solve all of your dilemmas. My hope is that you will add an understanding of personality styles to the other valuable tools you use in your parenting strategy. And no matter how helpful particular methods are, the core issue for any parent is carrying out Jesus' message to "love each other."[3] Understanding, accepting, and adapting to your children's personality styles is a way of loving your children in a very concrete way. The goal of this book is to help you deepen your love for your children.

PART I

Dealing the Hand

Chapter One

Did Someone Stack the Deck?

You've seen the scene many times in old Westerns. Our hero, usually clean-shaven and wearing a white hat, is playing cards in a noisy saloon. Across from him sit three men. They are unshaven, appear to need a bath, and are definitely not wearing white hats. Our fair and square man sees something he doesn't like. With eyes ablaze, he slams his hand on the table and whips his side arm from the holster. While the others quiver, he asks for a show of hands. As the cards tumble onto the table, our hero announces triumphantly—"I knew it, Dirty Bart! You're cheatin'. This deck has been stacked. Give me my money, or I'll blow your brain to the next county!"

Sometimes we parents feel like the hero in that Western. No matter how hard we try to be fair and square with our kids, we can't help asking, when it comes to one or more of them, "Did life stack the deck against us?" We look at one of our precious kids and say, "Where did he come from? Someone must have switched the tags at the hospital, because I could never be the parent of a child so different from me. Is this some trick? Why did I get dealt this hand? Can I throw in my cards and start over?"

I have some good news for you! You have been dealt a winning hand no matter how different your child's personality is from your own. God gives us diverse personalities within the family. The purpose of this book is to help you understand personality styles—yours, your spouse's, and your child's. And, to make the information as easy to remember and to use as possible, I will use the example of a card game and deck throughout this book.

So, if you . . .

♦ have a child who moves so slowly you would like to put a stick of dynamite under him,
♦ have a child who is so disorganized and fun-loving that you drive yourself crazy trying to help her get her life together,
♦ have a spouse who is so logical and precise that you feel like you are going to scream if you hear one more detailed explanation, or
♦ have a family member who is so overbearing and confrontational that the rest of the family feels intimidated,

. . . then read on.

In most families, personality differences are significant enough to cause major misunderstanding and pain. Take, for example, Janet, a wife and mother of three daughters. Janet, while rather quiet and reserved, has high expectations for herself and others. She is careful and meticulous, both in her personal appearance and in the appearance of her house. In fact, her daughters call her a neat freak!

Janet prefers order and routine and doesn't like any kind of confusion or chaos. Since she has very high expectations for her family, she is often disappointed in their performance. And since she is nonassertive, the family often runs roughshod over her wants and needs.

Enter Bridget, the youngest child—and believe me, when Bridget enters, everyone knows it. She bounces in with great exuberance. Bridget is excitable, often talking a mile a minute whether anyone is listening or not. Bridget's room is a disaster area. In fact, Janet has threatened to post a quarantine sign warning people to stay away for health reasons. Bridget's idea of cleaning a room is to stuff all her dirty clothes in drawers in order to distribute them later.

Bridget's world is fun, spontaneous, and positive. She loves people and people love her. In fact, the more friends, the better. Everything in Bridget's life is secondary to her relationships—including school, work, and duties around the home. When Bridget loses the approval of her friends, she is devastated. With Bridget around, nothing is dull!

Next, let me introduce Janet's middle daughter, Liesl, who believe it or not is even more spontaneous than Bridget. She seldom thinks anything through before acting. Her motto is, "Act now, think later—if at all." Liesl is continually surprising Janet with the "latest wrinkle." She has an absolutely delightful personality, and it is difficult to stay angry with her, even after some of her more disastrous capers. Like Bridget, she majors in people and having fun.

There is, however, a major difference between Bridget and Liesl—Dominance. Liesel is very strong willed with high ego strength. She is assertive, if not aggressive, and has a tendency to run roughshod over the rest of the family. If the parents draw a line, she puts her foot over it and challenges them to do something about it. Liesl would like to be the boss of the family, and indeed, at times it seems as though she is.

Heidi, the oldest daughter, is very different from her sisters. Steady, compliant, and a peacemaker, Heidi is concerned about doing the "right" thing. You can always depend on Heidi. Not a lot of surprises come from her. She prefers to think before she acts. When change is necessary, she wants to plan for it. She is conscientious but not a perfectionist.

Heidi is more deliberate in her approach to life than her sisters. She is also often slow to "get moving" in areas that her parents think are important. Janet and her husband often think Heidi could be more aggressive in certain areas of her life.

Now some of you already may feel sorry for Janet, the conscientious mother who wants to run a well-ordered household. But wait . . . there is a final card in Janet's hand—her husband. Wayne is outgoing and aggressive. He is a decision maker. He makes decisions for himself and for others if he feels they need help. But he is also impulsive and often makes those decisions without adequate facts. While Janet likes to weigh the pros and cons and not make quick decisions, Wayne wants to make decisions and get on with life. With projects around the house, Wayne wants to get the jobs done fast; Janet is more interested in quality. Oh, by the way, Wayne is also a bit messy. He has great difficulty putting things back where they belong!

No doubt you are feeling deeply for Janet by now—especially if your personality is similar to hers. Here is this wonderful woman who is desperately trying to maintain a well-ordered household, living with people who are just as intent on creating chaos. *What can she do?*

Janet is facing what many of you may face—the frustration of living with people whose personalities are very different from your own. I can personally vouch for the fact that the personality differences in the family have been irritating and stressful for Janet. I know because *she is my wife*. That's right. I'm the dominant husband she chose to live with. And in chapter 12—"A Winning Hand in Marriage"—I will show how personality differences have actually brought strength and vitality to our marriage of twenty-five years, and how you can develop these same qualities in your own marriage.

Learning to understand and accept personality differences can help strengthen your family relationships. It has certainly helped the Rickerson family. Janet has said, "I wish I had known about differences in personalities early in our family life. It has made so much difference in accepting the children, especially Bridget. I used to think something was wrong with her—or with me—but now I know it's just her personality style. I can accept that."

YOUR FAMILY PERSONALITY DECK

Every family has its own unique blend of four basic personality styles or, as I will call them, personality suits. As in a regular deck of cards, these four suits have thirteen cards each, every card having a different characteristic. Your family personality "deck" also may have four suits with thirteen "cards," or distinct personality traits, in each suit. (There *is* a joker! More on that later.) To help make this memorable, note that the first letter of each of these suits forms the acronym CARD. The four personality styles are:

> **C**onscientious
> **A**miable
> **R**elational
> **D**ominant

These make up your family personality deck. They are your winning hand! Here are brief descriptions of each personality style. Can you guess which one describes you and the others in your family?

Conscientious Personality Style
A person with a conscientious personality style usually is serious, reserved, accurate, systematic, perfectionistic, and interested in quality. One of the conscientious person's primary motivations is to do an excellent job in anything he does.

Amiable Personality Style
A person with an amiable personality style is usually steady, slow paced, controlled, cooperative, supportive, and a peacemaker. The amiable person's primary motivation is to be a loyal supporter in all relationships.

Relational Personality Style
A person with a relational personality style is usually emotional, optimistic, talkative, fun loving, impulsive, and people oriented. The relational person's greatest motivation is to bring fun and excitement into the lives of those with whom he comes in contact.

Dominant Personality Style
A person with a dominant personality style is usually strong willed, decisive, confrontive, impatient, independent, and results oriented. The dominant person, above all, wants to see results in anything he does.

By now you are probably starting to identify personality styles in your family. The personality inventories in the next chapter will enable you to determine more precisely the personality styles of your spouse, your children, and yourself.

COMBINATIONS

No one is exclusively one personality style. You will usually be more dominant in one of the four styles, but your actual personality is a combination of all four. Some of you may think, *I identify with the conscientious personality style most, but I also am a lot like the amiable personality style.* This doesn't mean you're psycho; it means you're a natural, almost equal, blend of two personality styles. You will exhibit the characteristics of both.

This can be confusing to yourself or to others, especially if the combinations are what I call conflicting. For example, you may take the inventory in the next chapter and find that you are a combination of dominant and conscientious. This means you will be impulsive in some situations but very cautious and predictable in others. Nothing is wrong with you. God has simply gifted you with a combination of two very opposite personality suits of nearly equal strength. Depending on the situation, one will emerge as more dominant than the other. Having conflicting personality styles can be an advantage. Once you're aware of your personality combination, you can use whichever suit best fits the situation. Here are the conflicting combinations and their distinctions.

Dominant/Amiable
When the dominant side is used, the person will be more decisive, impulsive, and less people oriented. When the amiable side is used, the person will be slower in pace, more deliberate in decision making, and sensitive to the people side of issues.

Dominant/Conscientious
When the conscientious side is used, the person will be very detail oriented. He will want everything to be just right. When the dominant suit is used, the person will be more impulsive. Getting the job done quickly will be more important than doing it carefully and perfectly.

Relational/Amiable
While the relational/amiable suits are both people oriented, one conflicting issue is pace. The relational side is very fast

paced; the amiable side is slower paced. The relational suit is also much more outgoing than the amiable suit. This means that according to the situation the person with this combination can sometimes appear very outgoing and spontaneous and at other times, more reserved and deliberate.

Relational/Conscientious
Several conflicting traits exist within these two suits. People with this combination have both an outgoing and a reserved side. They love being with people but still need substantial "alone" time. At times they appear to be very spontaneous; at other times they want everything to be planned.

If you or someone in your family has these conflicting styles, it will be helpful to remember how these combinations cause you or the other person to act differently in various situations. Again it does not mean there is anything wrong with you or the other person. It simply means that these personality suits are natural to that person, and he or she is usually subconsciously choosing the suit that fits the occasion.

LEARNING TO PLAY WITH THE HAND THAT HAS BEEN DEALT YOU

We all have been dealt a wonderful hand of different personality cards. We have the choice of allowing these differences to hurt or to help family relationships. We can build family relationships by learning to PLAY a winning hand. Following are four strategies, the first letters of which spell out the word *PLAY*.

Promote strengths
Limit weaknesses
Accept personality
Your compatibility

Promote Strengths

Each personality suit has its own wonderful blend of strengths and weaknesses. One important way that we can start playing successfully is to promote our family's strengths. Sometimes we are so focused on helping our children improve that we forget they need to hear just how special they are.

King David, who wrote many of the Bible's psalms, reminds us of each family member's uniqueness:

> You made all the delicate, inner parts of my body, and knit them together in my mother's womb. Thank you for making me so wonderfully complex! It is amazing to think about. Your workmanship is marvelous—and how well I know it.[1]

David praises God for the unique way He has made him. We can promote our children's unique personalities by attributing their strengths to God. Our children's basic personalities are fearfully and wonderfully made.

Limit Weaknesses

To be successes in life we must learn to limit our weaknesses. Successful people learn to capitalize on their strengths without letting their weaknesses stand in the way of success. We can help our children limit their weaknesses by working with them to strengthen areas that are keeping them from attaining their potential. For example, Bridget's strengths include a wonderful people orientation and a joyful approach to life. Her weaknesses include a rather unhealthy dose of disorganization. While actively promoting Bridget's strengths, Janet and I would be remiss as parents not to work with her on her weakness. To be effective in life, Bridget will have to become more organized. Although organization will never be one of Bridget's strengths, her tendency toward disorganization doesn't have to prevent her from reaching her life goals.

One of the major reasons God disciplines us through various situations is to strengthen areas where we are weak, to make us more like Him. We can cooperate with God to help our children limit their personality weaknesses and become successful followers and servants of Christ.

Accept Personality
Understanding and accepting the personality styles of our children starts by understanding and accepting our own style. *There are no inferior or defective personality styles.* One personality style is no better than another. We all have been uniquely gifted by our Creator, and each personality includes strengths and weaknesses. It takes a blend of all personality styles to make an effective society.

Sometimes the more outgoing, expressive personalities such as the relational style get a lot of press, but consider what the world would be like with all relationals. There would be a lot of fun and excitement, but wouldn't things get a bit chaotic? Where would we be, for example, without the consistent hand of the amiable person to stabilize situations and work steadily on projects? Or how would we feel if our surgeon was a highly dominant personality who said "that's close enough" when operating on us? Let's face it, it would be a very incomplete world if everyone was the same personality style.

Fortunately, God has created great diversity in people. God has created you just the way He wants you—with your own uniqueness. Based on this, you can accept yourself as you are, and you can accept your children as they are. You may feel weird at times—out of step with others—but you are normal.

We tend to accept ourselves more easily than we accept others, especially when others seem so different. When people think and act 180 degrees differently than we do, it's tempting to write them off as weird or defective. However, once we can accept the fact that people who think, feel, and act differently do not have personality defects, our relationships with others will improve dramatically.

Although it is a great challenge, accepting others is also a tangible demonstration of Christian love. The apostle Paul said, "Accept one another, then, just as Christ accepted you, in order to bring praise to God."[2] We bring glory to God when we accept our children's personalities.

As families, we can learn to blend individual personality differences into a corporate family personality. My family includes the wonderful humor and zest for life of Bridget, the quality control of Janet, the optimism of Liesl, the steadiness of Heidi, and the boldness of myself. We enrich one another's lives by the gifts of our diversity. We are a stronger whole because of the differences of the individual parts. Accepting one another allows blending to take place.

Your Compatibility

As you may already suspect, some personality styles are naturally more compatible than others. This does not mean that a parent who has a personality style opposite to that of his child will be a less-effective parent. It *does* mean there will be some natural differences that can cause conflict. This conflict can be minimized if the parent learns to play with a winning hand. A parent does this by accepting the natural differences in personalities and at times modifying his own personality to suit the needs of the child. We can do this without changing who we are.

I have learned to modify my personality at times to better suit the needs of others in my family. For example, if I am too dominant with family members, they get blown away by my aggressiveness and become resentful. I consciously lower my natural dominance at times with them. Janet lowers her perfectionism at times with members of the family. She realizes that to insist on her standards with people who see things differently is sometimes counterproductive. Modifying our personality styles does not mean changing our personalities, however. We will always be who we are, but we can change or modify behavior in certain situations for the benefit of other family members.

When we do this we are living out the meaning of the apostle Paul's words: "Love each other with brotherly affection and take delight in honoring each other."[3]

When we modify our behavior to meet the needs of a family member, we are giving preference to him in love. What a great idea!

Learning to PLAY with a winning hand can bring an extra dimension of joy to your family. I'm not saying that understanding personality styles is a cure-all or a final solution for all family problems, but it's certainly a key—a vital key that can unlock the door to family growth.

Chapter Two

What Suit
Are You Wearing?

To play a winning hand in parenting we need to know the meaning—the strengths and limitations—of the cards we've been dealt. Fortunately, the cards in the personality deck are quite distinctive. Once we are familiar with the four suits—Conscientious, Amiable, Relational, and Dominant—often, we can determine a person's personality suit by observation. For example, we can separate the conscientious and amiable from the relational and dominant personality types by observing whether the person is outgoing or introverted. If the person is more fast paced, then he is probably relational or dominant. To find out whether the person is relational or dominant, ask yourself if the person seems more people oriented or more results oriented. The relational person usually appears more talkative and lighthearted than the dominant person, who comes across as more intense and interested in getting results. As far as the conscientious or amiable types go, the amiable will generally appear more friendly and relaxed, while the conscientious will be more serious and reserved.

Another way to determine a person's personality style is by a forced-choice inventory, such as the one that follows. First, take the inventory on yourself and start becoming familiar with your own personality style. Next, either have your children take the personality inventory—if they're old enough (teenage and older because of the difficulty of the words)—or take the inventory for them by choosing the words that you believe best describe them.

I have included a children's personality inventory. This may be easier for you to use in determining your children's personalities than the adult version. I especially recommend using this inventory if your children are elementary-school age or younger. Chart the results of the inventory on the graphs to complete your family personality style deck.

Before you complete the inventories, I need to offer advice on interpreting the results. It is not uncommon for a person to be fairly close to the same score in three of the four personality style categories. If this happens to you, it does not mean you need to check into a mental hospital. You're normal! The most important score is the highest number. That number indicates your primary personality style. It is this style that you use in your relationships with your children and spouse.

If all four styles come out very close or if the style that comes out highest does not seem to be right for you, here are a couple of things you can do. First read chapters 3, 4, 5, and 6 on each of the personality style suits. As you go through each chapter, make a mark by each of the thirteen characteristics of that suit that seem to fit you. After you have completed the four chapters, add up the check marks. If the style with the most marks is different than the one on your graph and if the chapter seems to fit, this may be your primary personality style.

Another way to help determine your personality style,

when scores don't seem to fit, is to ask someone who knows you well to take the inventory for you. There are some who feel that this is an even more accurate way of determining personality styles. While that is not my view, having other objective opinions often can help a person who is struggling to determine his primary personality style.

ADULT AND TEEN PERSONALITY STYLE INVENTORY

On the adult and teen personality style inventory that follows you will find sixteen sets (labeled A through P) of words that will help you discover your personality style. In front of each word (reading across the page) is a line on which you are to put a number from 1 through 4. For example, set A has the words *exact, loyal, enthusiastic,* and *strong willed.* Place a 4 on the line beside the word you are most like. If you see yourself as being most loyal, then you would place a 4 on the line next to loyal. If you see yourself as being least strong willed, then place a 1 on the line next to that word. Complete a set by putting the numbers 2 and 3 next to the remaining words using the same criterion. (For example, if you placed 4 by "loyal" and 1 by "strong willed," you would put 3 by "enthusiastic" if that is more like you than "exact," to which you would assign the number 2.) In this example, your form would look like this:

A. _2_ Exact   _4_ Loyal   _3_ Enthusiastic   _1_ Strong willed

I suggest that you focus on how you act within the family as you take this inventory. Behavior can be different in various circumstances. Be sure to think of how you really are, not how you would like to be or how people expect you to be. Complete the sets, then add the numbers in each column and place the total in the appropriate space at the bottom. (Extra inventories have been included for use by each family member.)

ADULT AND TEEN PERSONALITY STYLE INVENTORY

Name: _____

	I	II	III	IV
A.	___ Exact	___ Loyal	___ Enthusiastic	___ Strong willed
B.	___ Critical	___ Steady	___ Expressive	___ Decisive
C.	___ Cautious	___ Consistent	___ Convincing	___ Must Win
D.	___ Follow rules	___ Peacemaker	___ Fun loving	___ Independent
E.	___ High standards	___ Diplomatic	___ People oriented	___ Impatient
F.	___ Serious	___ Slow to change	___ Promoter	___ Results oriented
G.	___ Chartmaker	___ Predictable	___ Cheerful	___ Brave
H.	___ Logical	___ Supportive	___ Inspiring	___ Confident
I.	___ Conscientious	___ Good listener	___ Popular	___ Leader
J.	___ Analytical	___ Gentle	___ Talkative	___ Dominating
K.	___ Organized	___ Controlled	___ Optimistic	___ Adventurous
L.	___ Researches facts	___ Deliberate	___ Impulsive	___ Outspoken
M.	___ Wants quality	___ Cooperative	___ Charming	___ Confrontive
N.	___ Concerned	___ Gracious	___ Emotional	___ Direct
O.	___ Reserved	___ Adaptable	___ Persuasive	___ Problem solver
P.	___ Systematic	___ Willing	___ Playful	___ Forceful

TOTALS

___   ___   ___   ___

ADULT AND TEEN PERSONALITY STYLE INVENTORY

Name: _____

	I	II	III	IV
A.	___ Exact	___ Loyal	___ Enthusiastic	___ Strong willed
B.	___ Critical	___ Steady	___ Expressive	___ Decisive
C.	___ Cautious	___ Consistent	___ Convincing	___ Must Win
D.	___ Follow rules	___ Peacemaker	___ Fun loving	___ Independent
E.	___ High standards	___ Diplomatic	___ People oriented	___ Impatient
F.	___ Serious	___ Slow to change	___ Promoter	___ Results oriented
G.	___ Chartmaker	___ Predictable	___ Cheerful	___ Brave
H.	___ Logical	___ Supportive	___ Inspiring	___ Confident
I.	___ Conscientious	___ Good listener	___ Popular	___ Leader
J.	___ Analytical	___ Gentle	___ Talkative	___ Dominating
K.	___ Organized	___ Controlled	___ Optimistic	___ Adventurous
L.	___ Researches facts	___ Deliberate	___ Impulsive	___ Outspoken
M.	___ Wants quality	___ Cooperative	___ Charming	___ Confrontive
N.	___ Concerned	___ Gracious	___ Emotional	___ Direct
O.	___ Reserved	___ Adaptable	___ Persuasive	___ Problem solver
P.	___ Systematic	___ Willing	___ Playful	___ Forceful

TOTALS

___ ___ ___ ___

ADULT AND TEEN PERSONALITY STYLE INVENTORY

Name: _____

	I	II	III	IV
A.	___ Exact	___ Loyal	___ Enthusiastic	___ Strong willed
B.	___ Critical	___ Steady	___ Expressive	___ Decisive
C.	___ Cautious	___ Consistent	___ Convincing	___ Must Win
D.	___ Follow rules	___ Peacemaker	___ Fun loving	___ Independent
E.	___ High standards	___ Diplomatic	___ People oriented	___ Impatient
F.	___ Serious	___ Slow to change	___ Promoter	___ Results oriented
G.	___ Chartmaker	___ Predictable	___ Cheerful	___ Brave
H.	___ Logical	___ Supportive	___ Inspiring	___ Confident
I.	___ Conscientious	___ Good listener	___ Popular	___ Leader
J.	___ Analytical	___ Gentle	___ Talkative	___ Dominating
K.	___ Organized	___ Controlled	___ Optimistic	___ Adventurous
L.	___ Researches facts	___ Deliberate	___ Impulsive	___ Outspoken
M.	___ Wants quality	___ Cooperative	___ Charming	___ Confrontive
N.	___ Concerned	___ Gracious	___ Emotional	___ Direct
O.	___ Reserved	___ Adaptable	___ Persuasive	___ Problem solver
P.	___ Systematic	___ Willing	___ Playful	___ Forceful

TOTALS

___   ___   ___   ___

ADULT AND TEEN PERSONALITY STYLE INVENTORY

Name: _____

	I	II	III	IV
A.	___ Exact	___ Loyal	___ Enthusiastic	___ Strong willed
B.	___ Critical	___ Steady	___ Expressive	___ Decisive
C.	___ Cautious	___ Consistent	___ Convincing	___ Must Win
D.	___ Follow rules	___ Peacemaker	___ Fun loving	___ Independent
E.	___ High standards	___ Diplomatic	___ People oriented	___ Impatient
F.	___ Serious	___ Slow to change	___ Promoter	___ Results oriented
G.	___ Chartmaker	___ Predictable	___ Cheerful	___ Brave
H.	___ Logical	___ Supportive	___ Inspiring	___ Confident
I.	___ Conscientious	___ Good listener	___ Popular	___ Leader
J.	___ Analytical	___ Gentle	___ Talkative	___ Dominating
K.	___ Organized	___ Controlled	___ Optimistic	___ Adventurous
L.	___ Researches facts	___ Deliberate	___ Impulsive	___ Outspoken
M.	___ Wants quality	___ Cooperative	___ Charming	___ Confrontive
N.	___ Concerned	___ Gracious	___ Emotional	___ Direct
O.	___ Reserved	___ Adaptable	___ Persuasive	___ Problem solver
P.	___ Systematic	___ Willing	___ Playful	___ Forceful

TOTALS

___   ___   ___   ___

PLOTTING THE PERSONALITY STYLE
INVENTORY GRAPH

Following is an example of how you will plot your personality style on the graphs on page 40.

Take the total from each column (I through IV) and enter it below the graph as shown on the example. The totals from this example, columns I through IV, left to right, are 19, 29, 60, and 62.

Take the total of your first column and make a dot on the vertical line under column C (I) on the graph. (The numbers from 16 to 64 on the left side of the graph will help you find the correct place.) Follow the same procedure with the letters A (II), R (IV), and D (III). Connect the dots and the graph is complete.

Circle the highest plotting point on the graph to discover your most dominant personality style. In the example, my personality style is D—Dominant, followed by R—Relational. Therefore, I would be called a dominant personality style.

ADULT AND TEEN GRAPH

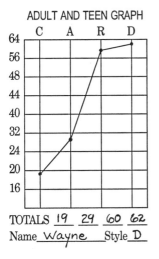

TOTALS <u>19</u> <u>29</u> <u>60</u> <u>62</u>

Name <u>Wayne</u> Style <u>D</u>

CHILDREN'S PERSONALITY STYLE INVENTORY

Instructions: The eight sets of words in this inventory will help you discover your child's personality. As in the adult and teen personality style inventory, put a number from 1 through 4 on every line in each set. For example, if you see your child as being most cautious, put a 4 on the line beside "Cautious." If you see your child as being least intense, put a 1 on the line by that word. Place the numbers 2 and 3 by the appropriate words.

Complete all eight sets of words and add the columns. Plot your child's graph on the children's personality style graph. (Extra inventories and graphs have been included so that both parents may rate each child.)

CHILDREN'S PERSONALITY STYLE INVENTORY

Name: _____

	I	II	III	IV

A. Do you consider your child most

____ Cautious   ____ Pleasant   ____ Playful   ____ Intense

B. You could see your child someday becoming

____ Accountant   ____ Counselor   ____ Salesperson ____ Boss

C. When your child plays, he or she usually focuses on

____ Doing things ____ Getting   ____ Having fun   ____ Leading and
     right   along   with play-   dominating
                                          mates

D. Your child works

____ Carefully   ____ Slowly with ____ Fast-paced   ____ Fast-paced
     by self   others   with others   by self

E. If someone took ten unposed pictures of your child, how would you
   describe the most frequent expression on his or her face?

____ Serious   ____ Warm   ____ Expressive   ____ Confident and
                                                              forceful

F. Your child's speech is usually most

____ Thoughtful   ____ Congenial   ____ Excited   ____ Direct

G. In school your child's teacher would consider him or her most

____ Careful   ____ Steady   ____ Talkative   ____ Impatient

H. The word that best describes your child is

____ Concerned   ____ Loyal   ____ Optimistic   ____ Confrontive

TOTALS

____   ____   ____   ____

CHILDREN'S PERSONALITY STYLE INVENTORY

Name: _____

	I	II	III	IV

A. Do you consider your child most

___ Cautious ___ Pleasant ___ Playful ___ Intense

B. You could see your child someday becoming

___ Accountant ___ Counselor ___ Salesperson ___ Boss

C. When your child plays, he or she usually focuses on

___ Doing things right ___ Getting along ___ Having fun with playmates ___ Leading and dominating

D. Your child works

___ Carefully by self ___ Slowly with others ___ Fast-paced with others ___ Fast-paced by self

E. If someone took ten unposed pictures of your child, how would you describe the most frequent expression on his or her face?

___ Serious ___ Warm ___ Expressive ___ Confident and forceful

F. Your child's speech is usually most

___ Thoughtful ___ Congenial ___ Excited ___ Direct

G. In school your child's teacher would consider him or her most

___ Careful ___ Steady ___ Talkative ___ Impatient

H. The word that best describes your child is

___ Concerned ___ Loyal ___ Optimistic ___ Confrontive

TOTALS

___   ___   ___   ___

CHILDREN'S PERSONALITY STYLE INVENTORY

Name: _____

I	II	III	IV

A. Do you consider your child most

____ Cautious   ____ Pleasant   ____ Playful   ____ Intense

B. You could see your child someday becoming

____ Accountant   ____ Counselor   ____ Salesperson   ____ Boss

C. When your child plays, he or she usually focuses on

____ Doing things   ____ Getting   ____ Having fun   ____ Leading and
    right   along   with play-   dominating
                    mates

D. Your child works

____ Carefully   ____ Slowly with   ____ Fast-paced   ____ Fast-paced
    by self   others   with others   by self

E. If someone took ten unposed pictures of your child, how would you
describe the most frequent expression on his or her face?

____ Serious   ____ Warm   ____ Expressive   ____ Confident and
                            forceful

F. Your child's speech is usually most

____ Thoughtful   ____ Congenial   ____ Excited   ____ Direct

G. In school your child's teacher would consider him or her most

____ Careful   ____ Steady   ____ Talkative   ____ Impatient

H. The word that best describes your child is

____ Concerned   ____ Loyal   ____ Optimistic   ____ Confrontive

TOTALS

____   ____   ____   ____

CHILDREN'S PERSONALITY STYLE INVENTORY

Name: _____

	I	II	III	IV

A. Do you consider your child most

___ Cautious ___ Pleasant ___ Playful ___ Intense

B. You could see your child someday becoming

___ Accountant ___ Counselor ___ Salesperson ___ Boss

C. When your child plays, he or she usually focuses on

___ Doing things right ___ Getting along ___ Having fun with playmates ___ Leading and dominating

D. Your child works

___ Carefully by self ___ Slowly with others ___ Fast-paced with others ___ Fast-paced by self

E. If someone took ten unposed pictures of your child, how would you describe the most frequent expression on his or her face?

___ Serious ___ Warm ___ Expressive ___ Confident and forceful

F. Your child's speech is usually most

___ Thoughtful ___ Congenial ___ Excited ___ Direct

G. In school your child's teacher would consider him or her most

___ Careful ___ Steady ___ Talkative ___ Impatient

H. The word that best describes your child is

___ Concerned ___ Loyal ___ Optimistic ___ Confrontive

TOTALS

___   ___   ___   ___

CHILDREN'S PERSONALITY STYLE INVENTORY

Name: _____

I	II	III	IV

A. Do you consider your child most

___ Cautious   ___ Pleasant   ___ Playful   ___ Intense

B. You could see your child someday becoming

___ Accountant   ___ Counselor   ___ Salesperson   ___ Boss

C. When your child plays, he or she usually focuses on

___ Doing things ___ Getting   ___ Having fun   ___ Leading and
    right   along   with play-   dominating
                                    mates

D. Your child works

___ Carefully   ___ Slowly with ___ Fast-paced   ___ Fast-paced
    by self   others   with others   by self

E. If someone took ten unposed pictures of your child, how would you
describe the most frequent expression on his or her face?

___ Serious   ___ Warm   ___ Expressive   ___ Confident and
                                            forceful

F. Your child's speech is usually most

___ Thoughtful   ___ Congenial   ___ Excited   ___ Direct

G. In school your child's teacher would consider him or her most

___ Careful   ___ Steady   ___ Talkative   ___ Impatient

H. The word that best describes your child is

___ Concerned   ___ Loyal   ___ Optimistic   ___ Confrontive

TOTALS

___   ___   ___   ___

CHILDREN'S PERSONALITY STYLE INVENTORY

Name: _____

I	II	III	IV

A. Do you consider your child most

____ Cautious   ____ Pleasant   ____ Playful   ____ Intense

B. You could see your child someday becoming

____ Accountant   ____ Counselor   ____ Salesperson   ____ Boss

C. When your child plays, he or she usually focuses on

____ Doing things   ____ Getting   ____ Having fun   ____ Leading and
right   along   with play-   dominating
                                   mates

D. Your child works

____ Carefully   ____ Slowly with   ____ Fast-paced   ____ Fast-paced
by self   others   with others   by self

E. If someone took ten unposed pictures of your child, how would you describe the most frequent expression on his or her face?

____ Serious   ____ Warm   ____ Expressive   ____ Confident and
                                                   forceful

F. Your child's speech is usually most

____ Thoughtful   ____ Congenial   ____ Excited   ____ Direct

G. In school your child's teacher would consider him or her most

____ Careful   ____ Steady   ____ Talkative   ____ Impatient

H. The word that best describes your child is

____ Concerned   ____ Loyal   ____ Optimistic   ____ Confrontive

TOTALS

____   ____   ____   ____

PLOTTING THE ADULT AND TEEN
PERSONALITY STYLE GRAPH

Plot the adults' and teens' personality styles on these graphs, following the directions and example on pages 32-33.

YOUR FAMILY PERSONALITY DECK: ADULT AND TEEN GRAPHS

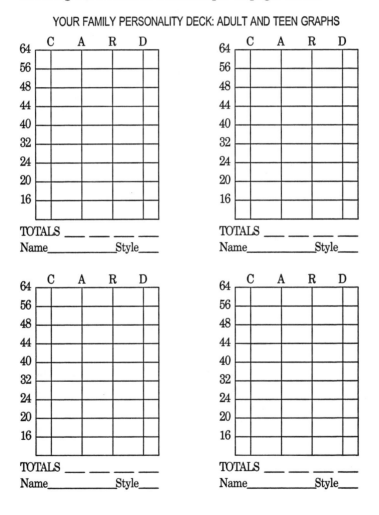

TOTALS ___ ___ ___ ___
Name_____Style___

TOTALS ___ ___ ___ ___
Name_____Style___

TOTALS ___ ___ ___ ___
Name_____Style___

TOTALS ___ ___ ___ ___
Name_____Style___

PLOTTING THE CHILDREN'S
PERSONALITY STYLE GRAPH

Plot each child's personality style on the children's graphs, which are provided below and on the next page. Follow the example given on page 33. If both parents completed a personality style inventory for each child, you can plot the results of both inventories and make a comparison of the two graphs for each child.

YOUR FAMILY PERSONALITY DECK: CHILDREN'S GRAPHS

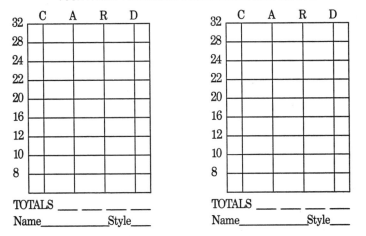

TOTALS ___ ___ ___ ___

Name_____Style___

TOTALS ___ ___ ___ ___

Name_____Style___

CHILDREN'S GRAPHS, continued

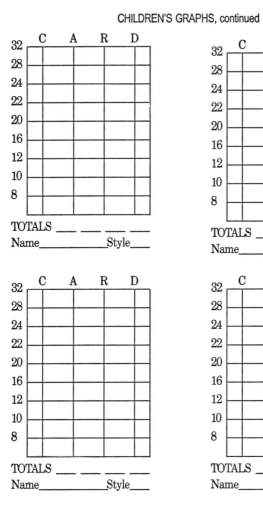

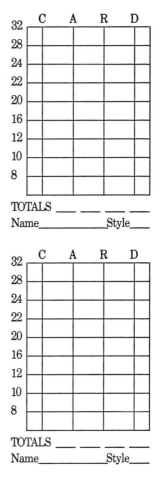

TOTALS ___ ___ ___ ___

Name_____Style___

TOTALS ___ ___ ___ ___

Name_____Style___

TOTALS ___ ___ ___ ___

Name_____Style___

TOTALS ___ ___ ___ ___

Name_____Style___

WHAT KIND OF DECK?

Now that each family member has taken a personality style inventory and charted the results on a graph, what kind of a CARD deck do you have? Who has the same kind of personality style in your family? Which family members are opposites?

I suggest that you have a family time together looking at the different personality styles in your family. Have each family member (who is old enough) share his graph. Ask other family members whether they see that person the way he sees himself. You might want to look back to the brief descriptions of the personality styles given on page 18. Discuss who in the family are alike and who are opposites in personality styles. What kind of frustrations do family members have because of differences in personality styles?

We have found it very helpful when the entire family understands personality differences. Sometimes when conflict occurs, family members will recognize that the conflict is caused by personality differences. Such comments as "Mom, your C (conscientious) is going off the graph, and it's driving me crazy!" or "Dad, lower your D, please," can defuse potentially explosive situations and actually have family members laughing at themselves.

The difference in the way the various personality styles approach life can really be quite humorous. For example, try to imagine individuals with different personality styles making that first appearance in the delivery room of a hospital. The relational baby looks around and excitedly says, "Isn't this great—look at all the people who are here for my birthday. Where's the cake? Let's have a party!"

The dominant baby, after getting over being angry about being slapped on his behind, scans the delivery room and says, "What's the deal here? Who's in charge? Where are my bags? I've got places to go and things to do. Move!"

The amiable baby emerges slowly, looks pleasantly at the doctor and nurses, and smiles wanly. "Hi, everyone," she says. "I love you all. I'm going to be a good baby. You all are going to like living with me. Is there anything I can do for you, Mom?"

The conscientious child cautiously peeks at his new world. Looking carefully at the delivery room, he notes every detail. After a few moments, with a serious look on his face, he says, "I'm a little concerned about the quality control in this delivery room. I notice some of the instruments have not been put back in their proper places. And was it really necessary to use those forceps? Doctor, how long has it been since you got your medical degree? What was your specialty? And by the way, who tied my umbilical cord? It needs to be a little tighter, and it's a little off center."

Understanding personality styles can be fun, but it can also be difficult and frustrating. This is not a precise science, even with the help of inventories. With very young children, whose personalities are still emerging, it is often difficult to discern styles. Keep watching and you will eventually be able to tell which styles are dominant.

Sometimes spouses will disagree on the personality style of a child. This may be because the child is a close combination of two styles. One spouse sees one style more clearly, while the other spouse sees another. If this happens, don't fight about it! Keep observing and perhaps get another opinion or two. You could even have someone, like a close friend or your child's teacher, do an inventory on your child. If it is still unclear, be patient. At some point you will be able to describe more precisely your child's personality style.

One reason why parents sometimes disagree on their child's personality is that the child is exhibiting what I call a social style. This child chooses to act in the way he believes is socially acceptable to his parents or other important people in his life. His personality takes the form of what he thinks is expected by others. Ignore this "social style" behavior and concentrate on major themes in the child's behavior that you see when no one else is watching.

Remember, whatever assortment of "personality cards" you have in your family, you've been dealt a winning hand! Personality differences can bring much richness and strength to your family.

Chapter Three

The Conscientious Suit

"I made the mistake one morning of asking my son how he slept the previous night," said the mother of a ten-year-old conscientious personality style son. "You wouldn't believe his answer."

"Well, Mom, I didn't sleep so good," the boy said. "I woke up at 1:02 and at 2:27 and at 3:05, and I finally got up at 5:00 and turned on the TV."

"Do you think I cared about the exact times he woke up?" the mom asked.

Many of us would agree with the mother. After all, who cares exactly what time a child wakes up? And what would make a child remember such things? A conscientious personality parent, however, would understand the child and think nothing of his reporting such details, because this is a very common trait.

In this chapter, we will look at thirteen "cards"—the behavioral tendencies of the conscientious personality suit.

CARD 1: DETAIL ORIENTED

A conscientious personality cares a great deal about details. In fact, noticing details is a routine part of life. Remember the example of the baby in the delivery room looking around and observing every detail and then, after careful observation, mentioning that the umbilical cord was not tied right?

Such focus on detail is not at all unusual for this one-fourth of the population. (The four styles are represented about equally.) It is these conscientious people who keep the rest of us in line. I was reminded of this at a recent seminar at McChord Air Force Base in Tacoma, Washington. I was speaking on personality styles and was telling the group about a time in another seminar when a conscientious participant mentioned to me that my belt buckle was off center, and it was bothering him.

As I told this story, I saw a woman look at her husband and laugh. I asked what was going on and the conscientious husband confessed, "Your tie tack is off center, and it's been bothering me all day."

CARD 2: PERFECTIONISTIC

The conscientious person is a perfectionist. On a scale of one to ten, with ten being perfect, the conscientious person expects the entire world to function at a ten level. Of the four personality styles, conscientious persons have the highest standards for themselves and for others. This means that they are often frustrated because life seldom measures up to a perfect ten.

Conscientious persons want to be perfect parents, perfect citizens, and perfect on their jobs. When they do not measure up to their own expectations, they often are hard on themselves.

Because of this perfectionism, conscientious persons often will not start a task unless they are sure they have the time and resources to do a perfect job. Others will sometimes see this as laziness or procrastination, but the conscientious personality simply dreads doing anything that he fears will not measure up to his standard of excellence.

You may have seen this trait in your child. You wonder why Susie puts off doing a paper or a book report. You think she is lazy or procrastinating, but in reality she is just a conscientious child dreading to start a task that she thinks will be difficult for her to do perfectly. Rather than do something halfway, she would rather not do it at all.

CARD 3: QUALITY CONTROL

Because conscientious persons have a great eye for detail and desire for perfection, they are excellent at quality control. Their high standards assure that products meet high standards of excellence. Often a dominant personality will create a product, an amiable personality will produce it, a relational personality will promote it, and a conscientious personality will check to make sure it has no flaws.

CARD 4: SERIOUS

It stands to reason that a person who believes the world, including himself, should be perfect will also be serious about life. Conscientious persons are generally more serious than the other three styles. Remember, they are committed to perfection in a not-so-perfect world. It's a staggering burden to observe a world that needs so much improvement!

Even in a young child you can often see this emerging seriousness. A conscientious child's face will show more concern than the faces of his more expressive relational or relaxed amiable brother or sister. Even in the preschool years, these children are embarking on a lifetime of concern over an imperfect world.

CARD 5: CAUTIOUS

When you want things to be perfect, you're going to be more cautious in your approach to life. Unlike the more adventuresome dominant and relational personalities, the conscientious person will carefully analyze the consequences of a situation before acting.

You can see this happening on a school playground. The conscientious child will stand at the side carefully observing other children playing a game before entering in. He will learn the rules, observe how well the others are playing, and assess his chances of not making a fool of himself. When the conscientious child is reasonably well assured that he can compete on the level of the others, then—and only then—will he play.

Relational and dominant personalities enjoy taking chances. Conscientious personalities would like to eliminate chance from their lives.

An example of these personality differences surfaced once between Janet, my conscientious wife, and my dominant self. We were about to celebrate our twenty-fifth wedding anniversary and had been talking about getting Janet another ring to complement her wedding bands. I mentioned to her that a person from my health club could buy jewelry wholesale from a dealer in San Francisco. He had offered to get an estimate for me but would have to take Janet's rings with him to the city.

My conscientious wife's reply was, "No way! If you think I'm going to let some stranger take my wedding rings to San Francisco, you're crazy. He might never bring them back. How long have you known this guy? Will he give you a security deposit? This sounds way too risky for me."

You can probably guess what happened. We went to a reputable, local dealer. Risk is out when it comes to my wife's rings.

CARD 6: NONASSERTIVE

Conscientious personalities tend to be nonassertive. Because of their perfectionistic nature, they often will have deep feelings and convictions about issues, but they will be reluctant to share these with others. They tend to avoid conflict by internalizing a lot of things. Conscientious persons will wait to share deep feelings until they believe it is safe or are about to burst from the pressure inside of them.

For example, a conscientious mother will want her family to help keep the house neat and clean. This cleanliness is very important to her, but even though she has feelings of frustration and resentment over the lack of cooperation, she will not share these feelings with her husband and children until she is furious. The conscientious mother believes her family should already know what she wants and do it without being told again.

CARD 7: ANALYTICAL

The conscientious personality seems to analyze almost everything. Logic and facts are very important. Perhaps you have tried to watch a TV show with a conscientious person. He will analyze what is happening and point out every inconsistency. You will hear, "How many bullets did he have in that gun? He's already shot twelve times and that gun only holds six bullets." Or "That's not realistic. She couldn't possibly have done all that in five minutes."

If you're like me, you will finally say, as I do to Janet,

"Why do you have to analyze everything? This is just a show. Let's just make believe and enjoy it."

CARD 8: DATA COLLECTORS

The conscientious personality will gather a lot of data before making a decision. He will check prices, features, and guarantees before making a purchase and then always wonder if he could have done better. Seeing an item advertised in the paper the next day at a lower price will convince him that he was hasty and not careful enough.

Conscientious persons have a tendency at times to gather too much information. At some point they become overwhelmed and confused by the data. This hampers their decision. The conscientious person has difficulty saying, "I've gathered enough facts. Now it's time to make a decision."

CARD 9: ORGANIZED

Lists and charts abound in the well-organized lives of conscientious persons. They are generally the most well organized of the four personality styles. While dominant and relational persons see organization as a hindrance to their spontaneous living, conscientious persons see it as a necessity and feel out of control when the day is not well organized.

On one occasion at a family conference, I asked family members to list what they would do if they had unlimited resources and freedom for one "perfect" day. One woman later confided in me, "You wouldn't believe how my husband organized his perfect day. Every minute was outlined from the time he got up until the time he went to bed. At 7:00 a.m. he showers and shaves. Eats a ham and egg breakfast at 7:30. Reads from 7:30 to 8:30. At 8:30 he goes to his woodshop and works on a project until noon. Everything about his perfect day was organized, almost to the exact second! And you know, that's how he really is. Sometimes it drives me and the boys crazy!"

While conscientious personalities can become too organized, they certainly do bring order to sometimes chaotic lives.

CARD 10: RESERVED

The conscientious person is usually more reserved than his more outgoing dominant and relational friends. You won't see a conscientious person bursting into a roomful of strangers and immediately making conversation the way a relational person would. The conscientious person would enter the room cautiously and stand off to the side and observe what was going on. Since the conscientious person does not enjoy small talk with strangers, he would try to be as inconspicuous as possible and blend into the group.

Conscientious personalities, as a rule, don't like to have attention brought to themselves. They much prefer to be in the background. Some teachers mistakenly think all children like to be honored in front of the entire class. The relational child thrives on such attention, but the conscientious child feels comfortable being recognized in a less conspicuous way.

CARD 11: THOUGHTFUL CHANGE

A conscientious personality resists change unless it is well thought out. Sudden and abrupt changes are not welcomed. For a conscientious person to feel good about change, the facts must be researched and there needs to be some assurance that the change is going to be good for all concerned. When the conscientious person is given advance warning of coming change and is convinced the change makes sense and fits into the big picture, then change will be accepted.

CARD 12: CREATIVE

Conscientious persons, generally, are quite creative. You will find many conscientious persons among the artistic, musical, and literary communities. Einstein, one of the creative geniuses of all time, was a conscientious personality.

CARD 13: CONSCIENTIOUS

A conscientious personality is, above all else, *conscientious*. He has a fine-tuned sense of what is right and wrong and tries to live by those standards. The conscientious personality believes that when there is a law you obey it, and when there is a policy manual you comply with it. I do need to mention, however, that the conscientious person becomes irritated with laws and policies that do not seem logical or consistent to him.

When conscientious persons are asked to do a task, they want to know exactly what is involved, so they can do the job thoroughly and well. They will ask a seemingly endless stream of questions before accepting an assignment.

I once asked a conscientious friend to teach one session of a four-part parenting class. I knew he was well qualified and would do an excellent job. I asked him to look the material over before making a commitment. He read it thoroughly and had all kinds of questions: "What does this mean? How could I possibly teach all this in one evening? This part needs more explanation," and so on. At one point I wanted to scream, "Why are you asking all these questions? Just teach the material. You don't have to work out every detail. You will do great."

But it was important to my conscientious friend to work out all the details. His inner voice said, "If you're going to do this, then you should do it right." Conscientious personalities want all the questions answered. They want to know the who, the where, and the why.

CONCLUSION

Conscientious personalities are the most likely of the four styles to feel that they are the only ones in the world like themselves. They often feel different and alone. They don't realize that over a quarter of the people in the world have personalities just like them.

If you are one of those conscientious personalities who feel alone in the world and maybe just a little weird, take heart. It's not so! History is full of great conscientious personality style persons. They are the CEOs of Fortune 500 companies, presidents of countries, famous scholars, and so on. Here are just a few we know and admire:

- Moses
- Eleanor Roosevelt
- Jimmy Carter
- Albert Einstein
- Linus
- Bill Walsh (ex-coach of the San Francisco 49er's)
- Tony Randall
- Prince Charles
- Elizabeth Taylor

Conscientious people bring great gifts to our world. Without their strengths our lives would be out of balance. The gifts that the conscientious personality offers include:

- Commitment to quality
- Analytical skills
- Preciseness
- An eye for detail
- Organizational abilities

Chapter Four

The Amiable Suit

Little Billy ambles out of his bedroom in the morning, one shoe on and one shoe off. He certainly doesn't look as though he's going to be ready to go to school in fifteen minutes. His mother says for the fifth time, "Billy! Hurry up and get dressed. You still have to eat breakfast. Why do you do this? I have to yell at you every morning."

Billy wonders what all the fuss is about. He moves the same speed every morning, but his parents are never satisfied. It seems to him he's moving fast enough. After all, he always gets to school on time. He wonders, "Why are people always in such a hurry?"

It seems the amiable child is never in a rush to do anything or go anywhere. His pace is slow, steady, and sure. For the faster-paced dominant and relational parents, this can be very frustrating. They don't understand a child who seems unaffected by time schedules.

The thing that saves the amiable child from the fury of his parents is his warm, amiable personality. This child is so winsome that it is difficult to stay angry with him for very long. Remember the amiable personality style baby in the delivery room, looking around and saying, "I love you" to everyone? That baby was alerting the world that he would be very easy to get along with.

Here are the thirteen cards in the amiable personality suit. Each card or trait represents a general behavior tendency associated with the amiable personality style. A person need not demonstrate all of these personality traits to fit the amiable personality suit. He will, however, exhibit many of them.

CARD 1: STEADY

You will not see a lot of ups and downs from the amiable person. Day in and day out his emotions seem pretty much the same. This is not to say that amiables cannot become emotional or have off days; but as a general rule, they are not given to great mood swings. They are steady.

Often a spouse will refer to an amiable marriage partner as his or her "rock." Relational or dominant personality styles often marry amiable people because of the stability they provide.

CARD 2: COOPERATIVE

The amiable person is usually very cooperative. Imagine for a moment four children in the same family representing the four personality suits. Here's what will tend to happen if you ask each child to do a chore for you. The dominant child's first response will probably be to argue and resist. The conscientious child will want to know the whole picture: exactly what you expect and why he has to do it. The relational child will give you an emotional response, arguing that he doesn't have time to do the chore and still play with his friends. The amiable child, however, might not want to do the chore but will cooperate because he wants to please you. Of the four personality styles, he will usually do what is asked with the least fuss.

CARD 3: GOOD LISTENERS

Amiable persons are noted for their ability to listen to others. While relational and dominant persons will do most of the talking, amiable persons will do most of the listening. They are valued friends because of this strength, but sometimes it works to their disadvantage. Amiables are such good listeners that others don't realize that they also need someone to listen to them.

This very thing happened between an amiable friend and myself. Jeff and I meet about every two weeks for lunch. We have the kind of relationship where we can share openly about anything we're going through. One day I realized Jeff was very upset with me. "You know, Wayne," Jeff said, "when you have something you need to talk about, I'm always there to listen. But when I have something I want to talk about, it seems that you're oblivious to the fact and keep talking about your interests."

This was a surprise to me, but as we talked further, I realized that Jeff was right. I often did not see that he needed to talk and would ramble on about my concerns.

I must add that not all spouses think their amiable mates are good listeners. In fact, sometimes the opposite is true. I have observed that the low-key, unemotional listening style of an amiable spouse is often interpreted by the other person as inattentiveness. This is especially true of women married to amiable men. It's not that these amiables are not listening, but that they're not responding as expected by their spouses.

CARD 4: PEACEMAKERS

Amiable persons do not like conflict, so they will work diligently to make peace. An amiable parent, for example, hates to see bickering and fighting in the family and will try to get feuding parties to stop. Sometimes the amiable parent will not tell his or her spouse of a problem with one of the children so as to avoid conflict in the family.

Amiable children will be mediators when playing with other children. They will often give up their rights to something to keep the peace—especially as they grow older. Heidi, our amiable child, was the peacemaker in the family, especially on trips, keeping peace between her sisters.

CARD 5: NONASSERTIVE

Given what we know about the steady, cooperative, listening amiable personality, it is logical to assume that he will also have difficulty being assertive. The very laid-back, peace-loving, people-oriented nature of the amiable makes it difficult for him to be assertive in relationships and tasks.

A dominant spouse will urge his or her amiable mate, "Why don't you just walk into your boss's office and ask for the raise? You have it coming." Or "Why won't you make a decision? You've been thinking about it for a month now."

Parents of amiables can become very frustrated with their child's lack of assertiveness. I can remember being very agitated with Heidi one summer because she would not immediately go out and look for a job. Finally, after what I thought was ample time, in a low-key discussion, I demanded that she find a job within a week. I am not recommending this as a parenting method, but it did help get our amiable child out into the working world.

CARD 6: QUIET LEADERS

Even though they are basically nonassertive, amiable personalities can become what is called the "strong, quiet leader." They have a way of moving up through companies—slowly and steadily—without much notice or fanfare. All of a sudden other employees look around and exclaim, "Where did Nancy come from? How did she get that position?"

Amiable personalities do not force their way to the top like the dominant personality or talk their way to the top like the relational person. They reach the top through their sure, steady work, loyalty to the organization, and likable ways. Amiables learn to be assertive when they need to be, but that assertiveness is often done in a congenial way. Sometimes when an amiable confronts you, it's so low-key you don't even realize what happened.

Some friends of mine observed this quiet leadership in their amiable son. "Chris was a leader," they said, "but always in the background. In fact, he got a special award one year for promoting harmony on the team."

CARD 7: SUPPORTIVE

Amiables are natural supporters of others. Since they don't feel the need to lead or dominate, they will only do so if given permission. Amiables are very happy in a supportive role, forever assisting those around them. I often hear parents saying, "Helen is so helpful. I wish all my children were that way," or "Nick seems so willing to help. How did you train him to be so helpful?"

It would feel nice to take credit for raising such helpful

children, but the truth is they're born that way. However, if you happen to be the parent of an amiable child and people keep telling you what a great child you've raised—don't show your hand! Let them attribute it to your superior parenting skills. The Lord knows we get blamed for enough negative things we had nothing to do with, so at times it doesn't hurt to take credit for something positive we had nothing to do with!

CARD 8: PLANNED CHANGE

Amiable personalities don't like sudden changes. They will change, but they like to plan for that change. Parents often don't understand their amiable child's resistance to sudden changes. A change of plans on a Saturday, for example, can upset such a child. "But, Mom, I was planning on playing with my friends and now you say I have to go shopping with you." The faster-paced dominant or relational parent might wonder what the big deal is about a little change of plans, but to the child who doesn't like sudden change, it's a very big deal. However, because amiables want to please, you may never find out just how much change bothers them. Amiables, whether children or adults, need time to plan for change.

CARD 9: GENTLE

Amiable people generally are very gentle in nature. They handle with care, so to speak, their personal relationships. If they have to confront you, they do it in such a way that you think they're paying you a compliment. Even when they are angry, they express their frustrations in such a way as to do the least amount of damage to the other person. Amiables always seem able to put themselves in the other person's place. They tend to treat others like they themselves would like to be treated—with tender, loving care.

CARD 10: LOYAL

Amiable people are known as very loyal to their friends and organizations. If treated at all reasonably, amiables will work faithfully for an employer for years. They wouldn't think of changing a job because, "After all, how could I change jobs when my company has been so good to me?"

Amiable people are liked by almost everyone, but they choose close friends carefully. The friendships they do have are in-depth and endure over long periods of time. Amiables are loyal friends who can be counted on.

CARD 11: PATIENT

While dominant and relational personalities do not know what the word *patient* means, amiables personify the term. Amiable children will sit for long periods of time absorbed with a project. They will work steadily and patiently, unlike their more impatient relational and dominant brothers and sisters.

Amiable persons have the ability to take the long look. While people around them are ready to quit, they keep on plodding steadily ahead thinking, *There's no reason to panic.* I'm sure an amiable must have made up the saying, "Inch by inch, anything's a cinch."

CARD 12: FAMILY ORIENTED

Walk into an amiable's office and you will find pictures of the family everywhere. They place great value on the family and family relationships. This is why amiables generally don't like work that infringes on family time or activities.

Amiable parents will work patiently in order to build a strong family. It's important to them to create a warm, loving atmosphere where persons have time for one another and enduring relationships can be built and nurtured.

CARD 13: AMIABLE

The term *amiable* sums up much of what we have been saying about this personality suit. *Webster's Dictionary* defines it as "having qualities that make one liked and easy to deal with or live with; good natured with a cheerful desire to please or to be helpful and sometimes a willingness to be imposed upon."

The amiable person is that and more.

CONCLUSION

Like each personality style, there are many notable amiable persons in all walks of life. Here are a few:

- ◆ Abraham
- ◆ Gerald Ford
- ◆ Tom Landry
- ◆ Perry Como
- ◆ Dwight Eisenhower
- ◆ Phyliss Ayers Rashad (who plays Clare on the "Cosby Show")

The amiable personality brings a great mediating balance to our world. The gifts that the amiable personality offers to us are:

- ◆ Steadiness
- ◆ Peacemaking
- ◆ Support
- ◆ Gentleness
- ◆ Loyalty

Chapter Five

The Relational Suit

Pam, the mother of a fourteen-year-old relational daughter, completely frustrated with her daughter's lack of forethought, said, "Diane, why don't you think first before acting?" Diane, in all seriousness, replied, "Because if I thought first I would miss all the fun!"

For the relational personality, fun is always important. In fact, sometimes it seems to be the only thing in the life of relational children. They have a great zest for life—it's something to be enjoyed to the fullest. The relational personality doesn't have time to sit around feeling depressed. The world is full of interesting people and exciting things to do.

Remember the little relational guy in the delivery room getting excited about all the people who had come to celebrate his birthday? Of the four personality suits, relational people are the celebrators of life, and they remind the rest of us that life is to be enjoyed. And the relational person offers us much more than joy, as we will see as we look at each of the thirteen cards in the relational personality suit.

CARD 1: EMOTIONAL AND DEMONSTRATIVE

Relational personalities demonstrate—with their eyes, with their body language, with their facial expressions, with their voices, with their very presence. Of the four personality styles, they are the most expressive.

You can pick a relational person out of a crowd by this expressiveness. Watch a group of people and you will often see one who seemingly cannot talk without using his hands. Every word has an accompanying gesture. His face is alive with expression when he talks—which is most of the time.

The relational person expresses on the outside what he is feeling on the inside. Sometimes this causes the more reserved amiable and especially the very private conscientious personalities to feel uncomfortable. A hug, a slap on the back, or any touch from a relational is not always understood or appreciated by others.

CARD 2: TALKERS

Relational personalities are famous for their ability to talk. Of the four personality styles, they are by far the most talkative. Most teenagers spend a lot of time on the phone, but it seems like a relational teenager has a telephone grafted to the side of his head.

I have given personality tests to groups of teenagers and noticed an unusual phenomenon among the relational girls. After the test when personalities are identified, the relational girls form a social group so they can talk together. They are so excited to find others who love to talk that they just can't wait to get together and start discussing their love for talking.

CARD 3: PERSUASIVE

The relational person is usually very persuasive. The well-worn saying, "He could sell a refrigerator to an Eskimo," was certainly thought of with the relational person in mind. They are usually among the most productive on any sales force.

Have you ever seen the stage or screen version of *The Music Man*? The male lead, the persuasive Professor Harold Hill, is a relational personality. He swaggers into River City, Iowa, to hornswoggle the citizens into believing he can teach the local youth how to play in a marching band. The truth is that the "professor" is not really a professor at all and cannot play a musical instrument or even read a single note of music. What he can do is persuade the people that he can indeed train their sons and daughters to become accomplished musicians and produce an outstanding band for the town.

While this story presents the powers of the relational person in the extreme, it is not unusual to see these charming people be very persuasive. When our relational daughter Liesl was six years old, she convinced a little neighbor girl that she was the mother of our eighteen-month-old daughter, Bridget. I couldn't believe my ears when my wife, Janet, told me this little girl had come to her and asked, "Is Bridget really Liesl's daughter?"

Although we sometimes hear stories of the negative side of a relational person's persuasive powers, many relational people persuade others to do very constructive things for our world.

CARD 4: UNORGANIZED

If you were to look in our relational daughter Bridget's room, you would find it a bit "disorganized." Now, granted, the rooms of teenagers with other personality styles can also look like war zones, but the relational teen really deserves the Medal of Dishonor here.

In Bridget's room, there's no place for anything and nothing has a place. When we ask her to clean her room, she thinks that means to stuff whatever is on the floor and her bed into drawers or in the dirty clothes basket (which is usually already overflowing).

I heard of another teenager with a novel way of cleaning his room. This resourceful relational boy would take the cover off the crawl space in his room and rake his belongings into it. After his mother had inspected his room, he would then dig the stuff back out as needed.

CARD 5: CENTER STAGE

Relational persons have a flair for the dramatic and enjoy the attention of being on center stage. As young children, they often will perform for appreciative parents and grandparents. In fact, if you show too much appreciation, they will want to go on forever.

This flair for the dramatic does not stop at childhood. Indeed, Janet and I have witnessed some unusual performances from Bridget during her teenage years. One incident we will never forget. Janet, Bridget, Liesl, and I were in Los Angeles, where I was speaking during the day at the National Conference on Families. One day while Janet and the girls were shopping, my wife realized that it was getting close to 6:00 p.m. She said, "We need to get back home because Dad will be waiting."

Bridget, in a loud, dramatic voice that could be heard by the clerk and other customers, said, "Mom, why do you keep hoping? Dad hasn't come home in seven years. Give up and quit kidding yourself. He's never coming back!"

Janet wanted to crawl out of that store to escape the kind looks of people who were sympathizing with this poor woman who had been deserted by her rat husband.

While you may never have to witness such an extreme performance, be prepared for the dramatic if you live with a relational person.

CARD 6: CHANGE ORIENTED

Change comes easily to the relational person. New ideas, new places, new challenges—all are welcomed. Because of their spontaneous natures, relationals do not see change as a threat. In fact, they are bored with routine. While the conscientious and amiable personalities resist sudden change, the relational person thrives on it.

CARD 7: ENTHUSIASTIC

Relational personalities approach life with great enthusiasm and don't understand the more laid-back lifestyle of the amiable or the cautious tendencies of the conscientious person.

When it's time to do something, they do it wholeheartedly. This enthusiasm is obvious to everyone involved with the relational person. Their expressive natures cause internal feelings of enthusiasm to be very visible to those they come into contact with. This enthusiastic approach to life balances the more low-key approach of the amiable and conscientious personalities.

CARD 8: INSPIRATIONAL

Because of their enthusiasm, expressiveness, and ability to persuade, the relational person can be very inspirational. Chuck Swindoll, the popular author, pastor, and director of

Insight for Living, is an example of a relational personality who inspires.

Each summer, a friend of mine takes his family to a week of camp sponsored by Insight for Living. Jerry, an amiable, comes back ecstatic. "It's an incredible week," he says. "I come away feeling like I can tackle another six months of life. It's the most fun and inspiring thing I ever experience."

From reading his books and listening to his tapes, I would assume that Zig Ziglar, one of the nation's most effective motivational speakers, is a relational personality. He is humorous, expressive, persuasive, and enthusiastic off the chart. He is paid large sums of money by businesses and organizations to inspire their members.

CARD 9: IMPULSIVE

Relational personalities often do things on impulse. Remember the girl who told her mother, "If I thought first, I would miss all the fun"? This teenager gives us insight into the spontaneous life of relational people. They often act first and think later. After all, if they thought first, a lot of the great opportunities for enjoying life would pass them by. To the relational person, this would be a disaster!

Relational persons often will buy things on impulse, agree to do things for others on impulse, and go places on impulse. While this trait is an integral part of their engaging personalities, it can cause them considerable remorse. The beautiful, exciting new sports car has to be paid for. The relational person suddenly realizes he does not have enough time to serve on the three committees for which he volunteered.

When our relational daughter Liesl was in high school, she rarely thought about anything before acting. Janet and I constantly seemed to be saying, "Liesl, if you had just thought before doing that, you wouldn't be in trouble." I do have some encouragement for those of you who have relational teenagers. They do become more disciplined as they mature. Liesl is now married and has two children. I am amazed at how much of that impulsiveness has been modified. She is still spontaneous but within limits.

CARD 10: FAST PACED

Think for a moment of some of the personality traits we have associated with the relational person: emotional, demonstrative, talkative, persuasive, change oriented, enthusiastic, inspirational, and impulsive. Put these all together and you have a very fast-paced person. It is sometimes difficult to even keep up with the thoughts of a relational person. Have you ever been talking to someone and started feeling anxious and physically tense? You probably felt like saying, "Slow down. I feel like I'm running a race and getting farther behind by the moment." By the time the conversation was over, you were exhausted. This is what it's like trying to keep up with a fast-paced relational personality.

Relational persons tend to talk fast, think fast, act fast, walk fast, and emote fast. For the slower-paced amiable and conscientious personalities, this can be irritating and pose a threat. But when kept in balance, the faster-paced relational persons help us all explore the wonderful opportunities of the world we live in a little more quickly. We can experience more of the abundance of life as we are swept along with their breakneck pace.

CARD 11: POSITIVE AND OPTIMISTIC

Relational personalities have an optimistic outlook on life. While a conscientious personality will often give three negative sides of a proposal, a relational person will give three positive views. This person believes that all things are possible and, in fact, probable. When trouble comes, relational people know that things are sure to get better.

I never cease to be amazed at the positive outlook of a good friend, Gary. We have been close friends since college days, and I can't remember a time when he has been anything but optimistic. When Gary calls me every six months or so, I'll ask, "How are things going?" The answer is always, "Great!" or at least, "Real good." Even when Gary is going through a crisis, he sees a silver lining in the clouds. He is always optimistic that things are about to get better.

Our relational daughter Liesl has this same optimistic outlook. I realized just how optimistic when a friend, Terry, left an ancient MG convertible in our garage that he was going to restore with his nine-year-old son, Danny. This was going to be Danny's "Christmas present." (I really think it was Terry's Christmas present to himself.) Terry asked me if he could store his father-son project in my garage until Christmas. I said, "Sure," expecting to see at least some semblance of a car. What Terry hauled into our garage was not recognizable at all. It looked like something left from a terrorist bombing in Beirut. This car was literally carried into my garage in parts.

I explained the situation to Bridget, but Liesl, a sophomore in high school at the time, was unaware of the arrangement. Bridget, wanting to put one over on her sister, said, "Liesl, Dad has a surprise for you in the garage. It's your birthday present." Liesl ran out to the garage and shouted, "All right! This is great! Daddy and I'll be able to put this together, and I'll have a great sports car."

Now what makes this story even more incredible is that I know absolutely nothing about cars. I have a zero IQ when it comes to mechanics. I feel it's a great accomplishment when I can change a tire successfully. Liesl knew all this, but still, with her eternal optimism, she believed that some day a sleek sports car would rise out of the scattered pieces of that junk pile. (What do you think a conscientious or amiable teenager would have said in that same situation?)

Relational persons don't understand people who don't share their optimistic view of life. They are bothered by pessimistic people and often will try to "jolly them up." While the relational person's optimism is a very positive trait, an overextension of this strength can become a weakness. Gary and Liesl sometimes do not deal with reality and get into difficult situations because of this blind spot. Sometimes it takes a conscientious personality to help the relational person look at a situation with a bit more objectivity.

CARD 12: DELIGHTFUL

I can truthfully say that living with two relational daughters has been delightful (most of the time). There obviously have been some frustrations, but overall the relational person is just plain delightful to be around.

Bridget and Liesl have brought a tremendous amount of fun into our family. Because of them, our family atmosphere has been more conversational, spontaneous, exciting, dramatic, and people oriented. Their charming personalities have helped Janet and me overlook some of the frustrations brought on by Bridget's and Liesl's unorganized, impulsive, and sometimes unrealistic tendencies.

CARD 13: RELATIONAL

I have heard it said that to relax, a relational person will snuggle up with a good book—and then invite five friends over to read it together.

Relationships are, indeed, the most important thing in the relational person's life. They are, above all else, people oriented. Relational persons like people and people like them. They generally have a lot of friends. Our house has been a center of social activity mainly because of our two relational daughters.

Friendships are so important to relational personalities that sometimes areas we parents believe are important—such as grades, chores, and family time—are assigned lower priorities than we would like. This can be very frustrating.

Because of the importance relational persons place on relationships, they are devastated by the lack of social approval. When their relationships are not going well, it is the one time in their life that they become depressed. It is this high people orientation that causes relational people to be among the most noticed and well liked in our society.

CONCLUSION

Notable relational personalities you might recognize are:

- ◆ Peter
- ◆ Bruce Willis
- ◆ Ronald Reagan
- ◆ Goldie Hawn
- ◆ John Madden
- ◆ Joan Rivers
- ◆ Liza Minnelli

The relational personality brings a real sense of joy and excitement to our world. The gifts that the relational personality offers to us are:

- ◆ Enthusiasm
- ◆ Inspiration
- ◆ Optimism
- ◆ Expressiveness
- ◆ Relationships

———————◆———————

Chapter Six

The Dominant Suit

Our daughter Liesl is a relational personality style, followed very closely by dominant. When she was still living at home, if she wasn't charming our socks off, she was trying to run the family. It was usually a battle of the wills to see who was going to be in charge.

In order to win a few of these skirmishes with Liesl, I was always looking for a new parenting strategy. I found what I thought would be a helpful idea in one of comedian Sam Levenson's books. Levenson told about his father giving the children the "evil eye," a scorching look that Sam's father would give the children when he was unhappy with them. Sam's father would not have to say one word. The "evil eye," as Sam called it, was all that was needed. The children would immediately fall into line.

I couldn't wait to try it out on my family. I thought, "What a great idea—I just look at my children, and they obey."

I tried the "evil eye" on them one at a time. I aimed it at Heidi, our amiable/conscientious daughter, when she disobeyed, and she dropped her head. I could see tears in her eyes. She immediately responded with repentance and changed behavior. I thought, *What a revolutionary new parenting technique. This is great!*

Next I tried my newfound skill on Bridget, our relational daughter. I directed my most scorching "evil eye" toward her, and she went into a comedy routine to try to break my concentration. Still, the "look" was moderately successful.

Finally I tried it on Liesl. When she misbehaved I looked at her with my most piercing "evil eye." She narrowed her eyes, threw back her own version of the "evil eye," and *I* began to cry! I was reminded that power is met by power when a parent has a child with high dominant traits. You nearly always have a nagging question in your mind, "Who's in charge?" At other times, there is no question—the dominant child is clearly in charge.

The baby in the delivery room who said, "Who's in charge, and where are my bags?" was giving fair warning to the world that another dominant personality was ready to take control. As we look at the thirteen cards, or characteristics, of dominant personality suits, we meet a pioneer who wants to find new frontiers—and then run them!

CARD 1: CONFIDENT

Whenever you are around a dominant personality you get the feeling he is confident—if not brash. It's not that the other personality styles lack confidence, but more that the dominant person seems to project that confidence to those nearby. Others sometimes see this ego strength as arrogance.

Now, a dominant person is not always confident or confident in all areas of life. Other factors, such as family life or other life experiences, often enter the picture. In fact, sometimes dominant persons can be quite insecure, but outwardly they will display a sense of confidence and high ego strength.

CARD 2: DECISIVE

The dominant personality makes decisions quickly and easily. In fact, he loves to make decisions—for himself and for others if they will let him. The dominant person has a difficult time understanding others, such as the amiable or conscientious personalities who are slower at making decisions, and will often see this more deliberate decision-making style as a weakness.

When Janet is slow or reluctant to make decisions, I can become frustrated. Where she sometimes considers too many facts, I, with my high dominant personality, will not gather enough data and sometimes make poor decisions. When Janet and I combine our strengths—her careful fact-finding and my decisiveness—we overcome our individual weaknesses and make better decisions.

CARD 3: CHANGE ORIENTED

While the conscientious and amiable persons are trying to keep the world the same, the relational and dominant persons are trying to change it. This can be very frustrating, but at the same time these differences can help maintain a good balance. Without the balance of conscientious and amiable persons, the dominant person will sometimes change things too fast without gathering appropriate data or considering the feelings of those involved in the change.

Dominant persons love change. They thrive on it. In fact, without change they become very frustrated. Dominant children become easily bored while playing. More than conscientious and amiable children, they constantly want something new to do. They relish sudden changes or new adventures the family might experience.

I can remember as a child enjoying the moves our family made. After living for seven years in a small eastern Washington town, I was excited when we moved to Los Angeles. The next year, when we moved to central California, I was again ready to go. In all, I attended four high schools in three states and basically enjoyed the changes.

A dominant spouse may desire change while his or her spouse may resist it. This causes tensions in the relationship. For example, Jean, a high dominant wife, may need a lot of change and challenge in her life. She might want to relocate, while her more amiable husband, Ron, is completely satisfied with living the rest of his life in the same city and working at the same job. Jean could feel frustrated by Ron's need for stability, and Ron could feel resentful and pressured by Jean's desire for change, a dilemma we will look at more closely in the chapter on marriage.

CARD 4: INDEPENDENT

People with dominant personalities are by nature independent. They like to work alone, relying on their own thoughts and abilities. Most children start asserting their independence in a very vigorous way when they're about two years old. Dominant children, however, continue to demand their independence throughout life in a more overt, aggressive way than the other personalities. They don't want help from their parents with homework and would do the homework themselves and receive a D rather than get help from their parents.

The dominant person is not a team person like the amiable personality. Consensus is not in his vocabulary. When Mike Ditka, the dominant personality coach of the Chicago Bears, took a team vote on whether to retain some of the replacement players after the 1987 strike, the team voted no. A day later, Ditka reversed the decision, saying that they didn't get where they are by taking votes. He'd keep the players he wanted to keep. So much for management by consensus with a dominant personality boss.

CARD 5: RESULTS ORIENTED

Dominant people always want to know the most direct route to the bottom line. They want results and not much else matters. They're most interested in getting the job done in the quickest, most efficient manner. Observe dominant personalities like President Lyndon Johnson, General George Patton, British Prime Minister Margaret Thatcher, and former Speaker of the House "Tip" O'Neill and you will see people cutting through the nonessentials to what produces results.

This desire for bottom-line results causes the dominant person to become very irritated when someone gives too many details or takes too much time talking about a problem. Take, for example, conscientious parents or teachers who explain in great detail to a dominant child what they want done. The child will become very frustrated because all he wants is a simple explanation.

You can also imagine the frustrations between a dominant spouse and his or her conscientious mate when it comes to working together. The dominant spouse just wants to get the job done quickly. The conscientious mate, while interested in doing the job well, could care less about how fast it is completed.

CARD 6: DIRECT

Results-oriented people will also be very direct in their communication. Think of Barbara Walters, a dominant personality, in some of her interviews. She will say, "Did you sleep with him?" not "How do you feel about the accusations that you slept with him?" or "Could you tell me about your relationship with so-and-so?" Barbara is so direct that the people she interviews are visibly shaken when she asks certain questions.

Dominant personalities not only deal directly with others, they prefer that others deal directly with them. They have little patience with the car salesman who will not give them a firm price on an automobile or tries to become their friend before selling them a car. They also become irritated by the conscientious salesperson who "bothers" them with all kinds of "unnecessary details." When asking directions, they just want the most direct route—not two alternate routes and five landmarks.

Dominant persons also want to be directly confronted in their personal relationships. In marriage, they will say, "Just tell me what's wrong. Why do I have to guess?" or "What do you want from me?"

CARD 7: IMPATIENT

Of the four personality styles, dominant persons are the most impatient. When talking to dominant persons, you can almost feel their impatience. You sense that you're on their time schedule and must be brief and not take up too much of their time.

A dominant person is too impatient to start at the beginning of a book or magazine—they randomly jump from middle to back to front. A dominant person doesn't have the patience to follow directions on products that have to be assembled. I have to force myself to start at the beginning of instructions. I invariably try to guess how something goes together, and when I have failed miserably, as a last resort, I will try to read the instructions or get someone else to put the monster together for me.

A few years ago on the day before Christmas, Janet and I

bought a stereo and entertainment center as a family gift. We were going to put together the "easy to assemble" entertainment center after the children went to bed on Christmas Eve. I took it out of the box and couldn't believe my eyes. There were millions of parts. It looked so simple in the picture. I panicked. I frantically called for my wife and said, "Look at this mess. We'll never be able to put it together. What are we going to do? It's too late to take it back." Janet graciously said, "Why don't you leave the room, if not the state, and let me try to figure it out." I came back later and she had all the pieces laid out, ready to assemble. I supplied some labor and in a reasonable amount of time the Christmas surprise was ready. A conscientious wife had saved her dominant husband from having a nervous breakdown.

CARD 8: FORCEFUL

Dominant personalities are very forceful. There is a certain intensity about the dominant person that can be intimidating to those around them.

I can tell you from life experience that sometimes we dominant persons use our forcefulness to gain control of situations or achieve results. But there are other times we don't realize how forcefully we are coming across. Many years ago a friend said to me, "Wayne, do you realize how you intimidate people? People agree with you to your face but are afraid to really be honest with you." I thought I was just being enthusiastic about changes I wanted to see made, but others were reading this as "Do what I say and don't ask questions." I had to learn to modify my behavior in that area.

CARD 9: COMPETITIVE

Each of the personality styles can become competitive in certain areas of life, but the dominant personality tends to be competitive in all areas. I have found that dominant persons are so competitive that they don't even like it that the letter D comes at the end of CARD because they want their personality style to be discussed first!

Dominant persons don't like to be second to anyone. They have a compelling desire to win at sports, on the job, and even on the highway.

CARD 10: PROBLEM SOLVERS

Give dominant persons a problem to solve and they're happy. After they have solved their own problems, they go around trying to solve everyone else's problems whether they ask for help or not.

Dominant people are known for their "quick solve" approach. Because of their ability to cut through superfluous data and look at the bottom line, they can often arrive at a suitable solution much faster than others. Sometimes their peers are amazed at the clarity and speed with which dominant persons can solve seemingly complex problems.

CARD 11: LEADERS

Dominant personalities are strong natural leaders. They try to take charge whether it's their right to do so or not. There is that inner drive to lead. Dominant persons will usually think they can do a better job of leading than the person in charge. They can respect another person's leadership, but that person must know what he or she is doing and be a strong, assertive leader. One of the greater tragedies to a dominant person is to see a designated leader who is not leading. This is the unforgivable sin!

While dominant people have great natural leadership abilities, their effectiveness is sometimes thwarted by a tendency to run over people. With more sensitivity to people and attention to the overall picture, dominant persons can increase their effectiveness dramatically.

CARD 12: ADVENTUROUS

I can imagine a lot of dominant personalities among the early pioneers. It would have required a thirst for adventure to face thousands of miles of hostile territory in the hope that you would find a better life in the new land. Conscientious persons would have wanted to know, "How accurate is the map? What exactly can we do to make a living? Is the trail safe?" The amiable person would still be in New York trying to make the decision, and the relational personality would want to know how many people were going on the wagon train. But the dominant person would say, "Who cares how accurate the map is? Don't worry about getting lost, we'll find our way. Let's just go—we'll worry about the details later." (The dominant person would be in real trouble, however, if a conscientious person did not draw the map and if one was not along to follow it.)

If you have a dominant personality child you probably fear for his life. Like the relational personality child, he seems to act first and think later. His love for adventure, it seems to us, will certainly lead him to an early death. We often wish he was a little bit less adventurous, so we could see him grow to adulthood and enjoy his own children.

CARD 13: DOMINANT

Add up all of the other cards in this suit and you have a comprehensive picture of dominants. There is really not much more to add. Dominant personalities, above all, have a need to dominate their world. Without a chance to dominate at least certain areas of their life, dominant persons become extremely frustrated. The success of dominant persons is usually the ability to balance their great leadership skills with an appropriate sensitivity to the feelings of people.

CONCLUSION

There is an impressive lineup of notable dominant personalities. A few are:

- ◆ Joshua
- ◆ Donald Trump
- ◆ George Patton
- ◆ Bill Cosby
- ◆ Mike Wallace
- ◆ Henry Ford I
- ◆ Lucy (of "Peanuts" fame)
- ◆ Barbara Walters
- ◆ Margaret Thatcher

Dominant personality people are important to our world because of their strong leadership tendencies and ability to produce results. Their gifts are:

- ◆ Ability to solve problems
- ◆ Ability to produce results
- ◆ Leadership abilities
- ◆ Pioneering spirit
- ◆ Directness

PART II

A Winning Hand in Parenting

Chapter Seven

Developing a Winning Hand

Every parent has a basic parenting style based on his or her own personality style. Our parenting styles impact our relationships with our children in significant ways. To develop a winning hand in parenting it is important to understand our own parenting style and how it affects our children. Before I offer advice on how to use your personality strengths to enhance your parenting skills, here are the four major characteristics of each parenting style:

CONSCIENTIOUS PARENTING STYLE

Conscientious
Conscientious parents want to be perfect parents and feel like personal failures when their children misbehave or do poorly in school. Conscientious parents will often blame themselves if the child does not measure up to parental standards.

Perfectionist

Conscientious parents want their children to excel in such areas as school, behavior, and athletics. These parents will expect their children to "know" what they should do without being told. Sometimes the conscientious parent feels the child's behavior is personally directed at him or her. This is because the conscientious person always wants to do what is right.

If a conscientious parent's child will not comply, the parent concludes that it must be because the child is mad or doesn't care about the parent. To the conscientious parent, this would be the only reason a child wouldn't do what was expected.

Logical

Conscientious parents will be very logical with their children. Some children will think their parent is obsessively logical and too prone to lecture and to deal in too much detail. Conscientious parents sometimes expect their children to think as logically as they do.

Nonassertive

Conscientious parents have high standards for behavior but will try to avoid conflict with their children. These parents will often store up resentment and then discipline in anger—or just give up.

AMIABLE PARENTING STYLE

Nonassertive

Amiable parents tend to be on the permissive side of discipline and often will not assert themselves to make their children behave. Amiable parents hope their spouse will take action or that the problem will go away on its own.

Peacemaker
Amiable parents want everyone in the family to get along and will stay in the middle to make peace. Relationships are important to them.

Steady
Amiable parents generally do not have measurable highs and lows. They are usually low-key and predictable in relationships with their children.

Supportive
Amiable parents are usually very supportive of their children. They don't put heavy demands on the children or expect them to live up to unrealistic standards. They want the children to succeed in areas important to the children.

RELATIONAL PARENTING STYLE

Impulsive
The relational parent will be inconsistent in discipline—sometimes strict, sometimes permissive. Follow-through is often inconsistent as well. Sometimes children will become anxious or frustrated with this characteristic.

Persuasive
The relational parent will use verbal skills to persuade children to do something and will sometimes overtalk to the point where the children ignore them.

Emotional/Demonstrative
The relational parent will be open and demonstrative with children. This parenting style includes emotional highs and lows.

Relational
For the relational parent, relationships with children are very important; a close, fun-loving family is highly desired.

DOMINANT PARENTING STYLE

Force of Character
The dominant parent will discipline with force of character, often intimidating children. Dominant parents often are not aware of how intimidated their children are by their forcefulness. Most children will submit from fear but will inwardly resent the parent.

Impatient
Dominant parents will want the children to obey immediately. They often have a "short fuse" and will discipline in anger.

Direct
Dominant parents will be very clear about what they want the child to do. The conversation is usually short, sometimes terse, but always to the point. The child has security in knowing where the dominant parent stands.

Dominant
Dominant parents have a tendency to want to dominate children, at times exercising too much control. They will become anxious with loss of control, especially in the teenage years. Most children will fight this control with either passive or aggressive behavior. The child who uses passive behavior might outwardly act very repentant and say he will do what the parent wants, but inside he is very angry. The anger will surface passively, for example, when a child just never gets around to doing what the parent wants but always says, "I'm

sorry, I just forgot." Another child might fight the dominant parent's control aggressively by arguing, yelling, or just saying, "I'm not going to do it."

A STRATEGY FOR WINNING

The first step in developing a winning hand in parenting is knowing our own parenting style. A second vital step is knowing our children's personality styles. The successful card player knows the cards in each suit well and when to play them. It is likewise very important for you as a parent to know the personality suits of your children well and how to skillfully use those cards. When you do this, you are playing with a winning hand.

Playing with a winning hand is an act of love. It takes great effort to be continually thinking of our children's personalities and how we can be sensitive to their uniqueness. It is much easier to do what comes naturally and let our children's cards fall where they may. When we play with a winning hand we are demonstrating the kind of love of which the apostle John wrote: "Little children, let us stop just *saying* we love people; let us *really* love them, and *show it* by our *actions*."[1]

The relational parent who understands that her perfectionistic seven-year-old conscientious son needs extra time to complete a task is playing with a winning hand. The dominant parent who, although bothered by his conscientious child's "why" questions, extends himself to answer those questions is also going to be a winner.

Whenever we tailor our parenting to fit our child's personality suit, we are following God's instructions: "Teach a child to choose the right path, and when he is older he will remain upon it."[2] The phrase "to choose the right path" refers to our child's "bent" or unique personality style. A paraphrase of this verse that includes this meaning is, "Remember his unique personality differences. Adapt your training to fit his needs and when he is mature you will see the results."

Four effective parenting strategies can be summarized by the acronym PLAY:

> Promote strengths
> Limit weaknesses
> Accept personality
> Your compatibility

Learning how to PLAY with these strategies will increase your parenting effectiveness significantly.

PROMOTE STRENGTHS

As we have seen, each personality suit or style has its own strengths or gifts and makes a special contribution without which the world would be incomplete. But sometimes we focus so much on the weaknesses of a personality suit that we ignore the specialness of each person. A child will then feel inadequate or defective in some way.

We can help our children feel good about themselves and pave the way for success in life by promoting their strengths, that is, by acknowledging on a regular basis those personality traits that are most obvious. For example, praise accuracy on a regular basis: "Jimmy, I've been noticing how careful you are in doing your math homework just right." To another conscientious child who asks a series of "why" questions, the parent could promote that strength by saying, "Heather, you always are so interested in knowing exactly what's going on. You certainly are a good thinker." In both cases the child feels validated because the parent has placed a positive value on a personality trait. The child might think, "That's good. I thought I was a little weird because I did that. I guess it's okay to be me."

LIMIT WEAKNESSES

We never want to try to change a child's personality, but we do want to help limit the weaknesses that go with each personality suit. We will not be able to eliminate our weaknesses nor our children's weaknesses, but to be successful, we often have to limit them.

For example, your dominant child might be overly aggressive and intimidate people. This weakness could affect the child's potential. I have known many people with great talents whose overaggressiveness has limited their success in life. People tend to react negatively to pushy people. To help your dominant child limit this weakness, watch for examples of aggressive behavior and start making the child aware of the consequences of such action. Give him some ideas on how he could modify his behavior so as not to appear so dominant to others. You could also point out examples of others being overly aggressive. Sometimes it's a shock—but a great learning experience—when we recognize our own behavior in someone else.

Often our children's weaknesses are an overextension of their strengths. For example, aggressiveness is a wonderful trait, but when overextended it becomes pushiness and intimidation.

ACCEPT PERSONALITY

Above all else we must accept our child's personality. Nothing is more devastating to a child than to feel rejected because he is different from his parents. A highly conscientious parent could easily give off signals to a relational child that he is not accepted because he's too verbal and flippant in his behavior. Parents, without realizing it, can say to a child by their actions, "You're not okay because you're not like me." One of the most profound verses in the Bible includes the phrase, "Accept one another."[3] The critical balance is to accept a child's personality suit while helping him limit his weaknesses.

YOUR COMPATIBILITY

As you have discovered by now, some children's personality styles are more naturally compatible with their parents' than others. (An amiable parent and an amiable child, for example, will probably have a basically smooth, mutually warm relationship.) Thus, there will be some areas of peace and some of conflict depending on personality likenesses and differences. In the following chapters we will look at the four parenting styles and the degree to which the personality styles of children are compatible or incompatible with each one.

MODIFYING OUR PARENTING STYLES

Once we understand our level of compatibility with a child, we can modify our parenting style to meet our child's needs. We can do this without changing our personalities. By modifying, I mean temporarily adjusting our actions or attitudes to match the personality needs of our children. We can do this when we know the personality suits of our children and play our cards thoughtfully.

For example, I have on occasion modified my dominant parenting style to meet the needs of our amiable/conscientious daughter, Heidi. She doesn't need forceful, directive input from me. On my better days, I adjust my normal style and become much more low-key with her. She needs to discuss things in a logical, nonthreatening way. She needs time to think things through and uses a lot of caution before changing. In my discussions with Heidi, I try to give her that time and space, and I work at relating at her pace rather than my own. When I do this, I remove the walls that often go up between us in conflict situations. She then feels understood and accepted and is much freer to respond to my input. I am still the same personality, but I have chosen to relate in a particular way that will build my daughter's sense of self-worth.

HANG IN THERE!

Remember, all this takes time. Don't become discouraged if you have difficulty putting the personality styles information into practice. Accepting your child just a little bit more is success. Being able to modify your personality at times for the needs of your child is success. Give yourself a break and pat yourself on the back when you put some of this information into practice instead of becoming discouraged when things aren't working perfectly for you.

A WINNING HAND IN SINGLE PARENTING

Before looking more specifically at how to PLAY with each of the four suits, I want to offer encouragement and some advice to single parents. In my counseling practice, I am continually reminded of the tremendously difficult job that single parents face in raising their children. I think there should be medals for single parents who have to be both mother and father while at the same time working diligently outside the home to support the family.

I find that single parents are always eager to learn new parenting skills, so here are some specific ways to use this material as a single parent.

Teach your child about his or her uniqueness. Sometimes during the trauma of a divorce or other loss of a parent, the child loses a sense of who he is and assumes different roles— such as the helper or mediator. At other times the child acts out his anxieties with behavioral problems. Your child needs to know he is a unique individual, loved and special just the way he is. Teaching your child the qualities of his own unique personality style is a way of helping him feel good about himself.

Share with your ex-spouse about your child's uniqueness. Share the information in this book with your ex-spouse. This will give the two of you common ground for discussing the child in a positive way.

Teach your children about one another's uniqueness. Sibling rivalry is sometimes an issue in single-parent homes. There just isn't enough of the single parent's emotional and physical resources to go around in the quantities that the children would like. Because of this they compete with one another for time and attention. One of the ways to diffuse this competition is to encourage them to understand one another's unique strengths and weaknesses. Use some of the ideas in chapter 12 to help your children be more understanding and tolerant of one another.

Remember, you're doing the best you can. Single parents reading this book are already doing a better job than most parents. I believe this is true because the single parents I have observed attending parenting conferences and reading books are very conscientious. Stop right now and give yourself a positive affirmation for being one of the few parents who care enough about their children to learn new information and skills.

Chapter Eight

Playing
the Conscientious Cards

Some parents were telling me about their conscientious child's Little League baseball game. "Shane struck out once during the game," they said. "Now, it will take him two days to get over it. He just gets so devastated about the smallest things. What's wrong with him?"

For openers, the parents did not really understand that what they were dealing with was, to a large degree, a personality style issue. Children, no matter what their personality style, can become very upset over not doing well in a sporting event, but the conscientious child will often respond as Shane did. Remember, that of the four styles, the conscientious personality has the highest personal standards. Shane had little tolerance for not doing what was expected—hitting the ball and getting on base. He was not just angry or disappointed. He was devastated because he had not performed perfectly and his performance had been witnessed by teammates and family.

Shane's parents can help him limit his weakness of being overly hard on himself, and encourage his wonderful strength of wanting to do well, by using the four PLAY strategies that I explained in the previous chapter. If you have a conscientious child, the information in this chapter can help you play with a winning hand. Again, here are the four strategies of PLAY:

Promote strengths
Limit weaknesses
Accept personality
Your compatibility

PROMOTE STRENGTHS

It is so easy to see the weaknesses of our children and often so difficult to see their strengths. And yet, we realize that positive reinforcement is one of the most effective ways of helping our children change. Your conscientious child has many wonderful strengths you can promote.

To assist us in promoting our conscientious child's strengths, let us review the cards in the conscientious suit.

- ◆ Detail oriented
- ◆ Perfectionistic
- ◆ Quality control
- ◆ Serious
- ◆ Cautious
- ◆ Nonassertive
- ◆ Analytical
- ◆ Data collectors
- ◆ Organized
- ◆ Reserved
- ◆ Thoughtful change
- ◆ Creative
- ◆ Conscientious

As you can see, the conscientious child has many wonderful strengths you can promote. Playing with a winning hand includes the important skill of helping your child feel special about who he is.

For example, when your child is laboring tediously over a

project, showing a strong desire to do an excellent job, you can promote the strength of quality control. Some parents, especially relational and dominant ones, might tend to say to the child, "Stop being so picky. You're never going to get your project done at this rate." A parent using the PLAY skills might say, "What a wonderful job you are doing on your project. You are spending hours getting it just right. I think it's great that you want to do things so well."

There are many opportunities to promote your children's strengths. If you have a conscientious child, take a moment right now to list two of his or her strengths on the parenting action plan (located near the end of the book, pages 167-174). This will help remind you to promote those strengths on a regular basis.

LIMIT WEAKNESSES

Although we all have received wonderful abilities and qualities, we have imperfections and weaknesses, too. God helps us limit our weaknesses through the truth about life we learn in the Bible and the power of the Holy Spirit. While we can never duplicate what God does for us in our children's lives, it is our responsibility as parents to help limit weaknesses we observe. We want our children to live up to their God-given potential, but without the growth that comes through confronting weaknesses, this probably will not happen.

For example, your conscientious child might be overly critical of himself whenever he makes a mistake. This is a weakness that could affect the child's success in life. His fear of making a mistake could make him depressed or afraid to do new things. To help your conscientious child limit that weakness, you could help him lighten up on himself when he makes a mistake. You could say something like, "Matthew, I know that you don't like to make mistakes, but we all make them.

It's okay to make mistakes. That's how we learn things."

At some point, a discussion of the people who have made great contributions to society after making multiple mistakes could be helpful. Talk about someone like Thomas Edison, who failed hundreds of times before inventing the light bulb. Or discuss Olympic gymnasts who fail at a routine thousands of times before getting it just right. Share an example from your own life of how mistakes have helped you in the long run.

Often our children's weaknesses are merely an overextension of their strengths. Here is a list of some of the strengths of the conscientious child, what happens when that strength is overextended, and what a parent can do to help the child limit that weakness.

STRENGTH ➤	WEAKNESS ➤	LIMITING THE WEAKNESS
Perfectionistic	Hard on self and others.	Encourage tolerance of self and others. Discuss unrealistic expectations. Praise his tolerance when you see it.
Serious	Depressed, gloomy	Encourage child to look at positive side of situations. Suggest actions when feeling down.
Careful	Won't take chances.	Encourage child to take appropriate risks. Ask, "What is the worst that could happen?" Remind child of good consequences when he has taken chances.
Reserved	Loner	Encourage interaction with others. Discuss uncomfortableness with people. Encourage joining groups and so on.
Analytical	Overanalysis	Give input when enough facts have been gathered. Encourage child to make decisions with less information. When becoming too detailed in conversation, suggest how to be brief.

Pick two weaknesses that you would like to help your conscientious child limit and write those on the parenting action plan. Decide what you will do to help your child limit each weakness and write it in the appropriate space.

ACCEPT PERSONALITY

The most important part of playing with a winning hand is the ability to accept your child's personality. There's nothing more discouraging to a child than to think, feel, and act in a certain way and then receive feedback from others that it's not okay to be who he is. A highly dominant parent could easily project that, because the conscientious child is not assertive, he somehow is defective. The relational parent could signal to the child that he's not acceptable because he's too quiet.

Turn to the parenting action plan and write what you will do to accept your child's personality.

YOUR COMPATIBILITY

Following is how the conscientious child responds to the four parenting styles.

Conscientious Child/Conscientious Parent
The conscientious parent wants the child to be perfect, and the conscientious child expects perfection from himself. Because both parent and child are perfectionists, they tend to get along well.

The conscientious parent needs to remember, however, that excessively high standards for both behavior and accomplishments may cause the child to outwardly comply and inwardly rebel. The child might become depressed or show passive-aggressive behavior, such as not doing a chore and saying he forgot.

Conscientious Child/Amiable Parent

The amiable parent's standards for performance are not as high as those of the conscientious parent, so the conscientious child will not feel as stressed with the amiable parent as he does with the conscientious parent. The child will try to live up to the amiable parent's expectations and not disappoint him. He might very well stifle feelings of anger toward siblings because he wants to live up to the parent's desire for peace.

The amiable parent needs to remember that the conscientious child doesn't want to disappoint the parent and will feel guilty if he does. The parent also needs to remember to express expectations in concrete terms. Remember, the conscientious child wants to know the exact what, who, and why.

Conscientious Child/Relational Parent

The conscientious child will be bothered by the relational parent's emotional/verbal approach to parenting. The child needs to know exactly what he is to do and why. The relational parent tends to be imprecise and inconsistent in discipline. The conscientious child will sometimes be frustrated by the emotional, expressive approach of the parent.

If the conscientious child sees the discipline as illogical, or if he cannot understand exactly what he is to do, he will become frustrated and might respond with outward compliance and inward rebellion. The relational parent needs to look for passive-aggressive behavior indicating the child's unexpressed anger or frustration.

Conscientious Child/Dominant Parent

The conscientious child can wilt under the sometimes stern and always direct discipline of the dominant parent. This child will outwardly comply with the dominant parent's force, but could conceal deep feelings of anger and bitterness.

The conscientious child wants to know the what of the rules

and the *why*. Dominant parents are frustrated by why questions and often will say, "Just do it—now! No more discussion!"

The conscientious child will have ambivalent feelings toward his dominant parents. On one hand, he will want to comply, and on the other, he will feel like rebelling. The rebellion is most likely to come out in passive-aggressive behavior or in consciously not doing a good job and saying, "I can't do it right."

———————————◆———————————

As you can see, the conscientious and amiable parenting styles are more naturally compatible with the conscientious child than are the relational and dominant styles. This is mainly because the conscientious and amiable personalities have a more predictable, slower-paced, less-assertive approach to life than do the relational and dominant personalities. This does not mean, however, that relational and dominant parents cannot be as effective with conscientious children as can the other styles. In fact, there is more individual stretching and growth in a relationship where people do not have high natural compatibility. It does mean, however, there will be natural conflict because less compatible personality styles have different ways of thinking, acting, and feeling toward each other.

MODIFYING OUR PARENTING STYLES

When we modify our parenting style, we change our natural tendencies for the moment to meet the personality needs of our child. Relational parents who slow themselves down and explain things in careful detail modify their parenting style for the conscientious child. While not easy, this is very effective and shows the child that we really care about his needs.

Here are two primary ways each parenting style can modify its behavior to meet the conscientious child's needs.

CONSCIENTIOUS PARENT

1. Lower expectations—Child has high energy, standards of his own.
2. Become more positive—Child will be helped by your positive attitude.

AMIABLE PARENT

1. Clear expectations—Child needs to know where he stands with you.
2. Encourage decisions—Child needs to move from fact finding to decision making.

RELATIONAL PARENT

1. Less expressiveness—Give child instructions with less words and more logic.
2. More discipline—Child needs structure in her life with few sudden changes.

DOMINANT PARENT

1. Less force of character—Child is sensitive and will withdraw.
2. Answer "why" questions—Child needs to understand why she is to do something and how it fits into the big picture.

COMPATIBILITY APPLICATION

Turn to the parenting action plan and complete the "Your Compatibility" section. Fill in what your natural compatibility is with your conscientious child and the characteristic that is most difficult for you to cope with. Decide on one thing you will adjust in your personality to better meet the personality needs of your child.

Chapter Nine

Playing
the Amiable Cards

I once asked a friend of mine whether, given another chance, she would do anything differently in raising her son Karl. Carol replied, "Now that we know about personality styles—that Karl is an amiable—I would help him see what a gifted personality style this is. I would want him to know what wonderful qualities he has. I didn't appreciate them when he was younger because I was always trying to push him into greater achievements. I didn't appreciate how easy he was to raise."

Appreciating the uniqueness of each of our children is what this book is all about. Those of you with young children have an opportunity that Carol and some of the rest of us didn't have. You can understand personality styles when your children are young and can play your cards better than we did. My hope is that you will start applying this information to your family life right now.

To help you learn to play the amiable cards, we will again use the four strategies in PLAY.

Promote strengths
Limit weaknesses
Accept personality
Your compatibility

PROMOTE STRENGTHS

What Carol was saying was that, if she had it to do over again, the one thing she would do differently would be to promote her amiable son's strengths. It is so easy to overlook our children's strengths while we are urging them on to greater accomplishments. There is nothing wrong with encouraging them to do their best or helping them work on their weaknesses, but this must be tempered with a good dose of positive reinforcement focused on the qualities that make them special. If we neglect this, our children can become driven adults who have little time to enjoy their uniqueness or accomplishments.

To assist us in promoting our amiable child's strengths, let us review the cards in the amiable suit.

- ◆ Steady
- ◆ Cooperative
- ◆ Good listeners
- ◆ Peacemakers
- ◆ Nonassertive
- ◆ Quiet leaders
- ◆ Supportive
- ◆ Planned change
- ◆ Gentle
- ◆ Loyal
- ◆ Patient
- ◆ Family oriented
- ◆ Amiable

From these cards you will find plenty of strengths to promote. By playing your cards right, you can help your children feel very special.

A parent can play his amiable cards well and help his child feel special by saying, "Debbie, I appreciate how well you play with your friends. You work hard at getting along with them. You are a very good friend."

Another parent might play her cards by saying, "Andrew, you're always so willing to help me when I ask. You don't even grumble. I appreciate that about you."

Promoting strengths over the lifetime of your children will help build their self-esteem. Your children will begin to see themselves as unique and worthwhile individuals. Look for the many opportunities that occur to play your amiable cards. If you have an amiable child, take a moment right now to list two of his or her strengths on the parenting action plan (located on pages 167-174 near the end of the book). This will help remind you to promote these strengths on a regular basis.

LIMIT WEAKNESSES

As we discussed in the last chapter, a child's weaknesses are often an overextension of strengths. For example, a strength of the amiable child is that he is steady. This steadiness, if carried to an extreme, can result in a lack of aggressiveness.

While the amiable child doesn't have a lot of ups and downs, there is not as much enthusiasm as is sometimes needed to accomplish a task. The steadiness becomes over-extended and acts like an anchor preventing the child from moving toward accomplishments.

Another strength that can become a weakness is the amiable's tendency to be a peacemaker. I can remember our amiable, Heidi, always trying to work out peace with her two sisters. In doing this, sometimes she was not assertive enough. She would reach her goal of peace, but at the price of not being honest with her own feelings. These feelings would then surface later with passive-aggressive actions such as nasty looks or snide comments toward her sisters. You can help your child limit this weakness by watching for this behavior and commenting when you see it. You could say, "Anne, I appreciate the fact that you always want to get along with your sisters, but sometimes I think you act like everything is okay when, really, you're still angry." You would explain why you think this is true and then encourage your child to not always seek peace at the expense of honesty.

Amiable persons are usually good listeners. People are attracted to them because of this strength. This strength becomes a weakness, however, when amiable persons do not share enough of themselves. It is not uncommon for amiable persons to become such good listeners that others fail to realize that at times they need someone to listen to them, too. Amiable persons often feel cheated when they have a problem and no one seems to notice or offer to listen.

You can help limit this weakness in your children by encouraging them to express themselves and their needs. Amiable children need to learn to become both givers and receivers.

Following are five strengths, the weaknesses that result from an overextension of these strengths, and how the parent can help limit those weaknesses.

STRENGTH —► WEAKNESS ————► LIMITING THE WEAKNESS		
Steady	Lack of assertiveness and enthusiasm.	Reward signs of enthusiasm and assertiveness. Encourage more assertive, enthusiastic behavior.
Cooperative	Cooperates at the expense of expressing own interests and ideas.	Draw your child's ideas out and praise him when he gives input of his own.
Quiet leader	So quiet that leadership vanishes.	Give your child encouragement, courage to lead within the family. Praise assertive leadership. Encourage him to become a more visible leader.

STRENGTH →	WEAKNESS →	LIMITING THE WEAKNESS
Plans changes	Resists change.	Praise times when child adapts to change quickly. When you notice child strongly resisting change, take time to discuss his feelings. Help him think through his resistance.
Loyal	Loyal to a fault—denial of faults.	Sometimes an amiable person is so loyal that he will overlook or deny things that need to be faced in a relationship or situation. While praising the strength of loyalty, help your child face denial when you see it. Discuss with your child his need to confront a friend or situation. Help him see that conflict can improve relationships and situations.

Pick out two weaknesses that you would like to help your amiable child limit and write those on the parenting action plan. In the appropriate space, write what you will do to help your child limit each weakness.

ACCEPT PERSONALITY

A balance between promoting strengths and limiting weaknesses provides a good foundation for your child's feeling of acceptance. I have observed that amiable children feel accepted by their parents because of their good natures and undemanding actions, but often feel rejected because they lack assertiveness. It is especially difficult for the more fast-paced relational or dominant parent to accept amiable children unconditionally.

Work diligently at accepting the amiable child with his strengths and weaknesses. You can help your amiable child realize that he is special just the way he is. The fact that he has weaknesses or weak areas is a natural part of life and should not detract from your unconditional acceptance of him as a unique and special person with the right to be who he is.

Turn to the action plan and write what you will do to accept your child's personality.

YOUR COMPATIBILITY

Following is how the amiable child responds to the four parenting styles.

Amiable Child/Conscientious Parent
The amiable child will respond well to the conscientious parent's discipline. While the child doesn't need all the details, he does need to know what is expected so he can live up to his role as a "good child."

The amiable child will not feel as pushed by the conscientious parent as he would by the relational and dominant parent, who are much faster paced.

The conscientious parent needs to be careful of overly high expectations for the amiable child. The child will want to please but may not always be assertive enough to attain the parent's high standards.

Amiable Child/Amiable Parent
The amiable child will feel well understood by the amiable parent. Both are slow paced, somewhat reserved, and agreeable. There is little in their personality styles that would produce conflict. However, the fact that the child has this affinity with the parent can cause jealousy among the other children.

The child might feel more secure with stronger discipline from the parent. Some of the child's needs can be overlooked by the parent because of the child's bent toward being the "good child."

Amiable Child/Relational Parent
The amiable child can feel frustrated because of the fast pace

of the relational parent. Because of the parent's "hurry up" style, the child can feel like he is constantly being hurried and become anxious.

The child can also feel overwhelmed by the rapid-fire verbal approach of the parent. The parent will want an immediate verbal reaction, but the child needs time to think and respond.

The emotional and sometimes inconsistent discipline of the relational parent can frustrate the amiable child, who wants predictability and peace at any price. The child might feel resentful toward the parent but will seldom confront. A positive factor in this relationship is that the child and the parent are both people oriented.

Amiable Child/Dominant Parent

The amiable child can feel "blown away" by the forcefulness of the dominant parent. Often the parent forgets that the child needs a gentle nudge, not an aggressive shove, to obey.

The amiable child will comply out of fear and will seldom confront the dominant parent. The parent might think all is going well and be surprised to hear that the child has stored up bitterness against the parent.

The parent often expects the child to be more assertive and faster paced. Because of this, the child can feel inadequate because of his more reserved approach to life.

———————◆———————

The amiable and conscientious parenting styles are most naturally compatible with the amiable child.

The amiable child finds it easier to respond to the slower-paced, more predictable, less-assertive amiable and conscientious parents. Let me remind you, however, that just because amiable and conscientious parents are more naturally compatible with the amiable child does not mean they will do a better job of parenting. Differences in personality styles can be overcome by a commitment to understanding and responding to the special personality needs of the child. When we modify our personality style, we can relate effectively with the person.

MODIFYING OUR PARENTING STYLES

We should never be expected to change our personalities, but we all can modify our behavior temporarily to deal effectively with others. A relational mother I know consciously modifies her behavior with her seven-year-old amiable son by not rushing him to get ready for school each morning. She has to bite her tongue because of the slow, deliberate way he goes about his morning routine. Modifying our behavior is never easy because it's contrary to our personality style. It takes a great deal of commitment and effort for a relational parent not to make her amiable child feel inadequate because he does not think, act, and talk as fast as she does. By the very act of modifying her behavior, the relational parent is saying, "I love you and accept you. We are very different, but it's okay for me to be me and you to be you."

Following are two primary ways each parenting style can modify behavior to meet the needs of the amiable child.

CONSCIENTIOUS PARENT
1. Lower expectations—The amiable child will feel guilt because of wanting to please his perfectionistic conscientious parent.
2. Clear expectations—Since the child wants to please, she needs to know what to do. Don't overdo logic and explanations.

AMIABLE PARENT
1. Discipline—The amiable child needs to know where he stands with you.

2. Encourage change—You are in the best position to help your child accept change more readily because you understand her fears.

RELATIONAL PARENT

1. Pace—Slow down your pace with your child. Walk in his shoes.
2. Discipline—Try to be more consistent with your discipline. Write down notes and refer to them often to recall what you said.

DOMINANT PARENT

1. Aggressiveness—Lower your aggressive approach. Talk less, listen more. Give your child permission to assert himself.
2. Patience—Although you hardly know what the word means, practice patience with your amiable child. Remember that while he might seem laid-back and nonassertive, he very well might pass by more aggressive people in a career or in other endeavors. For example, while the relational and dominant suits might aggressively push their way up the corporate ladder, they sometimes alienate people along the way. The more patient amiable person works at a slower, steadier pace but in the end gets further because of his amiable people skills.

COMPATIBILITY APPLICATION

Turn to the parenting action plan and complete the "Your Compatibility" section. Fill in your natural compatibility with your amiable child and the characteristic that is most difficult for you to cope with. Decide on one thing you will adjust in your personality to better meet the needs of your child.

Chapter Ten

Playing
the Relational Cards

Is there a joker in the deck? You'd better believe it! All the other suits have just thirteen cards, but we could easily add the joker to the relational suit. Those of you who have relational children are probably convinced that the joker has been wild in your family deck ever since the bundle of joy arrived.

With all the joy and humor that the relational child provides, there is an accompanying package of frustrations. Playing your relational cards wisely will help you keep a precarious balance between laughing and crying.

Some parents who do not know how to play the relational cards never accomplish this balance. These people go through life convinced they have been dealt a bad hand. I met a parent who believed this when I was giving a group of high school seniors the CARD personality assessment. The parent, a substitute teacher for the class, was only casually interested when

I administered the assessment to the students. As I began to give the characteristics of each personality style, I noticed the teacher was becoming very interested. The suspense was finally too great, so she asked if she could take the assessment. After discovering her personality style, she confided to me, "This is a real revelation. I am an amiable/conscientious. My husband is a conscientious/amiable. We have a daughter who is a conscientious/amiable. Her twin sister, who is sitting right over there, is a relational personality style. The rest of us thought she was just plain weird and highly irresponsible."

The mother went on to explain that they had plans for the twins to attend Stanford University. Both were smart enough to have a good chance to be accepted. The relational daughter, however, had started rebelling against the pressure. Instead of studying, she wanted to have fun—to be with her friends. "There is more to life than grades," she would tell her distraught parents. The pressure applied by the parents didn't do any good. To their dismay, she told them she would just as soon be a waitress as go to college. That was the final straw. Then they knew her wires were crossed.

Many relational personalities excel in academics. Stanford, I am sure, has its fair share. The problem with this girl was that her parents were not playing a wise hand. The girl was reacting against their lack of understanding of how to play the relational cards. They thought the only game in town was played with amiable and conscientious cards.

Once again review the strategy for playing a strong hand in parenting:

Promote strengths
Limit weaknesses
Accept personality
Your compatibility

PROMOTE STRENGTHS

I'm afraid Janet and I often did a poor job of promoting the strengths of our relational daughter Bridget when she was young. We were focused on what she was not doing; she was showing off and embarrassing us with her unorganized life-style (we called it irresponsibility in those days).

I'm sure Bridget heard the message loud and clear that it was not okay to be herself. Now in all fairness to parents, it sometimes is difficult to focus on a relational child's strengths when you have just broken your leg falling over a toy he left out or suffered serious emotional trauma from a brief sixty-second visit to your teenager's room.

But strengths there are, and we need to promote these on a regular basis. Let's review the characteristics of the relational suit.

- ◆ Emotional
- ◆ Talkers
- ◆ Persuasive
- ◆ Unorganized
- ◆ Centerstage
- ◆ Change oriented
- ◆ Enthusiastic
- ◆ Inspirational
- ◆ Impulsive
- ◆ Fast paced
- ◆ Positive and optimistic
- ◆ Delightful
- ◆ Relational

What a list! Just look at the selection of strengths to promote. The teacher we talked about earlier could say to her relational teenage daughter, "You know what I really appreciate about you? You are so much more people oriented than the rest of us in the family. That's a great quality."

Something I really appreciate about our daughter Bridget is that she is fun to be around. Bridget is rarely moping about, looking at what's wrong with the world. She loves life and lets everyone know it. It's contagious. I can promote that strength with Bridget by saying, "Bridget, I really enjoy being around you. You're up and positive and that helps my attitude."

With a small child, you could say, "Steve, you're always so happy. I like that!" There are many cards in the relational suit that you can use to promote strengths. If you have a relational child, take time now to list two strengths on the parenting action plan (located near the end of this book, pages 167-174). Begin promoting at least one of these strengths immediately.

LIMIT WEAKNESSES

The relational child's weaknesses are usually as obvious as the strengths. With our daughter Liesl, the weakness that bothered us most was her impulsiveness. She would often act first and consider the consequences later. It seemed like we were constantly saying, "Didn't you think of the consequences? Didn't it occur to you what would happen?" Her answer was always, "No." One way to help relational children limit their impulsiveness is to make sure they suffer the consequences of their impulsiveness. Don't bail them out, or you will reinforce that weakness.

With our relational daughter Bridget, we've worked on the weakness of her lack of organization. Since a relational child is not usually organized in thought or action, it is wise for parents to help limit that weakness. A parent can help by working with the child to structure homework, establish schedules, organize his or her bedroom, and set a budget when old enough. It is important, however, when working with the relational child, to remember that this is a personality style weakness and very difficult to overcome. Expect your child to improve, but don't place your expectations too high.

Don't forget that these two weaknesses are strengths that have been overextended. Impulsiveness and lack of organization are part of what makes relational persons spontaneous. The spontaneity makes them a delight to be around. When the impulsiveness and lack of organization are overextended, however, those characteristics become weaknesses.

Following are five strengths of the relational child, the weaknesses that result from overextension, and how the parent can help limit those weaknesses.

STRENGTH →	WEAKNESS ─────→	LIMITING THE WEAKNESS
Talker	Talks too much, doesn't give others a chance to express themselves.	Point out others who do this. Give your child input when he talks too much. Role play with you being the relational person and your child as an amiable.
Positive	Lack of reality, overcommitment.	When child becomes overly optimistic, help him face reality. Ask questions, "What will it take to do this?" "What are the facts?" "Exactly how will you get this done?"
Fast paced	Careless, leaves others behind.	Discuss with child the mistakes that result from moving too fast. Show child how to slow down and proceed in a more steady manner.
Relational	Spends so much time with people that other things get neglected.	Discuss consequences of work not done because of excessive people contact. Help child develop discipline in this area by scheduling balance between people and work.
Emotional	Big mood swings, overemotional at times.	Discuss consequences of mood swings, talk about ways of keeping emotions on a more even keel.

Pick out two weaknesses you would like to help your child limit and write them on the parenting action plan. Write the actions you will take.

ACCEPT PERSONALITY

As charming as relational children can be, it is sometimes difficult to accept them. With Bridget, we often focused so much on what we saw as her responsibility that at times she felt unaccepted by us. It helped Janet and me greatly to finally understand that there were many other relational children with Bridget's mix of charm, humor, enthusiasm, carelessness, and disorganization.

The personality styles that usually have the most difficult time accepting the relational person are first the conscientious and next the amiable. We all need to remember, however, that to enjoy the delight of the relational child we must tolerate just a little frustration. Turn to the action plan and write what you will do to accept your child's personality.

YOUR COMPATIBILITY

Following is how the relational child responds to the four parenting styles.

Relational Child/Conscientious Parent
The relational child's spontaneous and unorganized spirit is likely to drive the conscientious parent crazy. Likewise, the child will feel extremely frustrated by the parent's perfectionism and likely will become exasperated by the parent's logical and detailed explanations.

Relational children don't understand the conscientious parent's negative and reserved approach to life. They are likely to call this parent "boring."

The child may resist any overcontrol on the part of the parent by verbal "crazy making"—that is, attempting to divert the attention from an uncomfortable subject to something less threatening. When child and parent have conflict, often the parent will either blow up or give up in frustration.

Relational Child/Amiable Parent
The relational child's style is much faster than his slower paced amiable parent. Because of this, the child often will want the

parent to respond much faster than the parent feels comfortable with and will feel frustrated with the parent's desire for planned change and a more reserved approach to life in general.

Relational children, however, have an easier time relating to the amiable parent because both styles are very people oriented. The relational child needs the amiable parent's more unemotional, steady parenting—but will not admit it. The amiable parent needs to become more of a disciplinarian with the relational child, helping him structure limits for himself.

Relational Child/Relational Parent

The relational child and the relational parent get along very well together. Both are emotional, fast paced, verbal, and like to have fun. And fun they will have.

While all the fun is going on, however, sometimes the parent doesn't help the child develop self-discipline and the ability to stick to the task. Although the child will fight structure, he actually will feel anxious and out of control if the parent doesn't provide it.

The relational parent and child will confront one another —often emotionally and loudly. Then they make up fast—and have fun again.

Relational Child/Dominant Parent

Relational children will feel intimidated by the dominant parent's controlling parenting style. They want more freedom than the dominant parent is willing to give and will rebel against parental control by becoming even more unorganized and "irresponsible."

Relational children do like the dominant parent's fast pace and desire to change. They may choose to approach this parent—rather than an amiable or conscientious parent—for permission to do something because they feel the dominant parent is likely to make an impulsive decision in their favor.

MODIFYING OUR PARENTING STYLES

Conscientious parents usually have the most difficulty modifying their personalities to meet the needs of the relational child. This is because of the great difference in the two personalities. *However, it can be done.* I have watched my conscientious wife, Janet, modify her parenting style to better meet the needs of our two relational daughters. It hasn't been easy for her. A part of Janet acknowledges that there are normal personality differences between her conscientious tendencies and the relational personalities of Liesl and Bridget. But another part of Janet resists some of those differences. "If they were just more organized," she will say, or "Why don't they think before acting?"

I have seen Janet modify her personality style by using less logic and shorter explanations than normal when communicating with Liesl and Bridget. She works hard at making quicker decisions because of the needs of our relational daughters. She is also less cautious with the girls, not because she feels less cautious, but because she's willing to adjust her personality to meet their needs.

Following are two primary ways each parenting style can modify behavior to meet the needs of the relational child.

CONSCIENTIOUS PARENT
1. Less caution—Relational children need freedom to be spontaneous and adventuresome. They thrive on change.
2. Less logic and concern for detail—Approach relational children with briefer, less logical instructions. They won't remember all the details anyway.

AMIABLE PARENT

1. Quicker response—Work at increasing the pace at which you respond to your child's requests.
2. More emotion—Your relational child will see your low-key response as a lack of interest in her exciting world.

RELATIONAL PARENT

1. More structure—Remember that while you and your relational child will resist structure, your child still needs a balance from you.
2. Slower pace—At times, slow your pace down a little to help your relational child learn to slow his pace at the appropriate times.

DOMINANT PARENT

1. Lower dominance—Try to maintain a balance for firm parental discipline while permitting the child flexibility in many areas.
2. Higher tolerance—Your relational child's lack of results in areas you deem important can cause conflict. Remember, people are more important than productivity to the relational child.

COMPATIBILITY APPLICATION

Turn to the parenting action plan and complete the "Your Compatibility" section. Fill in what your natural compatibility is with your relational child and the characteristic that is most difficult for you to deal with. Decide on one thing you will adjust or modify in your personality to better meet the personality needs of your child.

Chapter Eleven

Playing
the Dominant Cards

Picture it. Los Angeles, 1950. A diminutive five-foot, fifty-year-old graying lady is pursuing her skinny thirteen-year-old son with a yardstick. She has visions of swatting him on the rear because of his defiance. He has frustrated her beyond her level of tolerance (which is very low to start with), and she is attacking with the only weapon available. The son, who towers over her at a mighty five feet eight inches tall and 130 pounds, takes the yardstick away and says, "Don't ever try that again."

The mother, realizing her bluff is over, makes the well-known statement of surrender, "Wait till your father gets home." The boy thinks, *No sweat. Dad won't be home for two months.*

The preceding is a true story between a dominant mother and her dominant son. I can verify it because I was the dominant son. My mother was one of the many parents who gets the strange feeling that someone else in the family thinks he can do a better job of being in charge than she can. Parents of dominant children have the very special challenge of raising a strong-willed child. This chapter is to help you dominant parents play your cards wisely.

One of the problems is that dominant children don't play by the rules of the game. They make up their own rules as they go to gain an advantage. While there are no "card tricks" to help you with your dominant child, knowing how to play dominant cards can help improve your odds significantly.

Most parents can tell at a very early age when a child has high dominant tendencies. They can even sense that emerging force of character at the early ages of two or three. The child is not highly people oriented unless either his amiable or relational suits are also high. He is bored easily and wants to get things done quickly but usually with little concern for quality.

As a dominant child, I can remember always wanting to dominate—to be in charge—to be first. I found it very frustrating, believing as I did that I was destined to run the world, to realize that no one wanted to be bossed around by a three-foot-tall child. Not even my peers were excited by my desire to be in charge. I soon realized that to survive I must lower my dominant tendencies and raise my second highest suit, the relational. I found in most cases that relational tendencies were more acceptable to others than dominant ones.

While it can be very frustrating to be the parent of a dominant child, let me remind you that we, like other personality styles, have significant gifts. I can remember being frustrated as a child because those gifts were not always appreciated. Even as an adult, sometimes we dominant personalities get bad press. I can understand why, but we need to have our strengths acknowledged as well. It is the "I can do anything" tendencies of the dominant personality that help keep our world moving ahead.

A year or so ago I heard about a five-year-old dominant child moving ahead a little faster than was appropriate. Perhaps you read the story. The boy decided to take his two-year-old sister for a ride in the family car. After driving for several miles, the boy saw the red lights of a police car behind him and dutifully pulled to the side of the road.

When the policeman asked the boy what he was doing, he matter-of-factly replied, "Taking my sister for a ride." At the police station the boy was told his parents were going to have to come pick him up. "But I have the car," the boy replied. "Do you want me to go get them?"

While this story runs chills up the spines of most parents, we have to admire the positive attitude of this child. If you have a dominant child, remember that he is capable of such adventures. Read on to learn the strategy for playing the dominant cards:

Promote strengths
Limit weaknesses
Accept personality
Your compatibility

PROMOTE STRENGTHS

Often the dominant child's strengths are not promoted because they are not seen as positive characteristics. I think it is especially important for parents of dominant children not to get so caught up in power struggles that they fail to praise the child for his special gifts. Here is the list of characteristics:

- Confident
- Decisive
- Change oriented
- Independent

- ◆ Results oriented
- ◆ Direct
- ◆ Impatient
- ◆ Forceful
- ◆ Competitive
- ◆ Problem solvers
- ◆ Leaders
- ◆ Adventurous
- ◆ Dominant

"Erin, you're willing to try just about anything," says a mother to her seven-year-old daughter. "That's good. A lot of people are afraid to try new things."

Erin's mother is promoting a basic strength of the dominant child. Instead of saying, "That's too hard for you," or "Don't try things you can't do well," the mother is focusing on an area of giftedness. The child feels good because a basic characteristic of her personality has been validated.

"Chad, I was noticing today what a good leader you're becoming," says ten-year-old Chad's father. "Your friends seem to respect your leadership abilities." Another, less discerning parent, in a similar situation might say, "Chad, it sure seems like you're bossy with your friends," or "Quit trying to tell everyone what to do. People don't like that."

Dominant children are decision makers. Obviously, as children, they're going to make a lot of mistakes. Some of their decisions will be impulsive. As a parent you can focus on the poor decisions or on the good decisions. I'm not saying to ignore all poor decisions. There does need to be a good balance, however, between promoting strengths and limiting weaknesses.

Look for the good things your dominant children do. Reinforce those strengths that are a unique part of their personalities. Notice that the thirteen dominant cards listed earlier can be perceived either as weaknesses or strengths. Make a decision to major in strengths and minor in weaknesses. When children feel good about themselves, they are much more open to our input about improving their weak areas.

If you have a dominant child, take time now to list two of his or her strengths on the parenting action plan (located on pages 167-174 near the end of this book). Begin promoting at least one of those strengths immediately.

LIMIT WEAKNESSES

The bad press we dominant personalities sometimes receive comes primarily from our low people orientation and our focus on quick results. While we are taking the most direct route to an accomplishment, we often leave a few bodies strewn along the way. This does not make us popular.

I learned a little later than I should have that I had to be more sensitive and less results oriented if I was going to be successful. Over the years I have worked hard at becoming more sensitive to other people's pace and feelings. Sometimes under pressure I fall back into some bad patterns, but overall I think I have attained a reasonable degree of balance.

This balance is what you want to help your children achieve. In the process of helping them limit their weaknesses you do not want to squelch the very traits that make them special. You want them to realize it is okay for them to be who they are, but to be successful in life, they must modify some of their behavior.

The dominant child who fails to limit his assertiveness will be avoided by other children. The dominant child who wants to make all of the decisions will soon be doing just that—but there won't be any other children around to follow those decisions.

Following are five strengths of the dominant child, the overextension of which will limit the child's success in life.

STRENGTH ⟶	WEAKNESS ⟶	LIMITING THE WEAKNESS
Confident	Arrogance, cockiness.	Help child see himself through others' eyes (this is often a blind spot for dominant children). Give examples of how he could act differently in a situation. Discuss examples of how his cockiness affects relationships.
Decisive	Makes impulsive decisions or makes decisions for others.	Allow child to suffer consequences of impulsive decisions. Praise well-thought-out decisions. Show child how to gather facts and evaluate before acting.
Independent	Isolation, won't work with others.	Give child feedback when you observe her becoming overly independent. Discuss accomplishments that have been made by teamwork. Give projects that involve teamwork and then offer feedback.
Results oriented	Poor quality, running over others.	Show consequences of results without proper attention to detail. Help child work out a structured approach to achieve results that includes attention to details and quality. Point out examples of what happens when results become more important than people.
Direct	Insensitive, blunt, hurts people's feelings.	This is another blind spot, so give child feedback when he is overly direct with people. Explain that, while this seems natural to him, others need a softer approach. Role play the way he sometimes approaches people and then suggest an alternative, less blunt way.

ACCEPT PERSONALITY

I can recall feeling unaccepted during most of my early years. I don't think the rest of the world really knows what to do with the forcefulness of the dominant personality, especially in children. My advice to you as a parent is to give a lot of thought to those characteristics that often seem like liabilities but are really assets. By seeing these personality traits in a more positive light you can feel more accepting toward your child, and your child will certainly feel more accepting of himself.

Turn to the parenting action plan and write what you will do to accept your child's personality.

YOUR COMPATIBILITY

The dominant child is more naturally compatible with the dominant and relational parents. Here is how the dominant child responds to the four parenting styles.

Dominant Child/Conscientious Parent
The dominant child will overpower the conscientious parent, wearing him down with his force of character. The child may see the parent as weak.

The child often sees the parent as nitpicking, always wanting him to do better with more care and detail. He will react against the parent's detailed explanations and "why" questions, thinking instead, *Just tell me what you want me to do.*

The child's free spirit and need for change and challenge will go against the parent's need for a more orderly, cautious environment.

Dominant Child/Amiable Parent
The dominant child also will overpower the amiable parent. This parent, however, will not struggle as much as the conscientious parent will because of lower expectations and a desire for peace. The dominant child won't understand the parent's concern over his failures to get along with siblings and peers. He will also be frustrated by his amiable parent's slower pace

and more deliberate, cautious decision making.

While outwardly complying with the amiable parent's loving discipline, the dominant child might inwardly rebel.

The parent will be somewhat overwhelmed by the faster-paced, change-oriented, pioneering dominant child.

Dominant Child/Relational Parent

The dominant child will respond well to the relational parent's high energy and change orientation. Both are impulsive. But, he will be frustrated by the parent's lack of consistent discipline; he wants to know what is required, even though he will resist complying.

The dominant child also will react negatively to the verbal overkill of the relational parent.

Dominant Child/Dominant Parent

The dominant child and dominant parent will understand each other quite well, but they also will go head to head in a struggle for control at times. The parent might "win" in the early years but will become extremely frustrated during the child's adolescence as he realizes he is losing power and control. The child often will comply outwardly but rebel inwardly—frequently finding alternate ways to do what he wants.

The dominant child will appreciate the dominant parent's fast pace, succinct explanations, and encouragement to meet challenges and explore new horizons.

MODIFYING OUR PARENTING STYLES

As you can see, conscientious and amiable parents will have more differences with the dominant child than do their dominant and relational counterparts. As a result, the conscientious and amiable parents will face a greater task when modifying their personalities to meet the needs of the dominant child.

Following are two primary ways each parenting style can modify behavior to meet the needs of the dominant child.

CONSCIENTIOUS PARENT
1. More succinctness—The dominant child needs to know clearly and simply what you want him to do.
2. Allow pioneering—The dominant child needs challenge, new frontiers, things to accomplish.

AMIABLE PARENT
1. Respond quickly—The dominant child needs a quick response to her questions and requests.
2. More assertiveness—The dominant child responds to assertiveness and does not understand a parent who does not take charge.

RELATIONAL PARENT
1. More consistency—A dominant child wants to know where he stands with the parent.
2. Fewer words—A dominant child gets frustrated with long stories, explanations, and instructions.

DOMINANT PARENT
1. Lower dominance—Try to stay out of power struggles with a dominant child. For example, a dominant parent who is trying to get his six-year-old child to clean up his room by intimidation might change to a more amiable approach. This could be to sit with the child, lower the voice and body language intensity (no finger shaking), and explain how important it is to clean the room and what the consequences will be if he does not.
2. Manage anger—A dominant child becomes angry

when a dominant parent "blows up." Work at managing your anger (remember you already look intense). Uncontrolled anger will frighten even the dominant child.

COMPATIBILITY APPLICATION

Turn to the parenting action plan and complete the "Your Compatibility" section. Fill in your natural compatibility with your dominant child and the characteristic that is most difficult for you to cope with. Decide on one thing you will adjust in your personality to better meet the personality needs of your child.

PART III

Other Winning Hands

Chapter Twelve

A Winning Hand in Marriage

One of the scariest things that happens in our marriage is when Janet and I decide it's time to wallpaper a room. Choosing the wallpaper is not too bad. Janet decides. The problems begin when we start work. We gather the equipment together and I say, "Let's get this over with. If we start now we can be done by noon."

Janet replies, "This is not a race. We are going to do a good job."

The old anxious feeling starts to overcome me. *This could be a long day,* I think to myself. "Well, honey, let's start here in the middle of the room," I say to Janet. "Give me that panel, and I'll slap it up."

"Wayne Edward [when my wife says my middle name, I know the pot is beginning to boil], you do not 'slap' wallpaper up in the middle of a room. Let's start somewhere else and make sure that it matches first."

137

"What difference does it make if it matches?" I reply. "I thought that's what pictures and drapes were for. If it's really bad, I'll stand in front of it."

My last statement is an ill-timed joke, and Janet is not amused. She informs me that my services are no longer needed. She will phone a friend who is interested in quality. "Something," she says, "you obviously have never heard about."

I am slightly offended but delighted to be released from a situation that had all the potential for ending our marriage—on the spot. *Besides that,* I think, *I now have some vital information to pass on to the couples I counsel: Never, ever, hang wallpaper together if one of you is a dominant personality and the other conscientious.* I feel good about the thousands of marriages I'm going to save with that one insight.

THE CARDS WE DRAW IN MARRIAGE

As parents we are dealt the personality cards of our children. We have no choice in the matter. In marriage, however, we ostensibly have some control. Or do we? (Have you ever wondered why you married someone so different from yourself?) It's not that we were playing blindfolded, but our choices sometimes seem rather strange, wouldn't you say?

DO OPPOSITES REALLY ATTRACT?

The reason so many of us marry opposites isn't easy to understand. What is clear, however, is that opposites do attract. The problem is that many times opposites do not keep on attracting.

Here is what often happens. We meet someone who has qualities much different from our own. We enjoy being around that person because we enjoy the differences. For example, a quiet, reserved amiable might be attracted to an outgoing relational. The amiable enjoys the expressiveness of the relational.

The amiable has always wished he could be more expressive and now finds he can vicariously experience expressiveness through his relational friend. The relational person, on the other hand, often feels a need for more stability. This person feels grounded and secure around the steadiness of the amiable. The two people sense that through the merging of these two personalities in marriage, they will complement one another and bring a certain completeness to their relationship.

This attraction happens during stage one of a marriage: *romance.* The feelings are so strong that they distort the couple's vision of all the cards in the suit. The vision starts clearing, however, in the second stage of the marriage, which I call *reality.*

DO OPPOSITES KEEP ON ATTRACTING?

During the *reality* stage, the opposite traits begin to be viewed differently. The spouse who enjoyed the expressiveness of the relational partner now begins to be increasingly bothered by the impulsiveness that is also a part of that suit. "Why doesn't he think before acting?" "Why does she always want to be going somewhere?" "Why do we always have to be around people?"

The relational spouse is also beginning to be irritated by the less expressive partner. The "rock" will now not move. "Why does he not want to talk?" "Why doesn't she ever act spontaneously?" "It takes him forever to make a decision." "This marriage is getting boring."

All these thoughts, questions, and frustrations can cause the person to conclude, "I married the wrong person. We are incompatible." Is the marriage really incompatible, or is the couple just facing the *reality* of marriage? Differences can add vitality and enjoyment to marriage, and those same differences can also be irritating at times. What produces variety and enjoyment in relationships also produces tension.

ARE WE INCOMPATIBLE?
CAN OPPOSITES KEEP ATTRACTING?

Incompatibility is a controversial issue, but it is my belief that people do not have intrinsically incompatible personalities. Rather, they *choose to be incompatible*. Let me explain. By now, we have seen that some personality styles are more naturally compatible than others. For example, amiable and conscientious personality styles usually get along very well together because of their similarities. There are fewer differences, so in that way they are more naturally compatible.

On the other hand, many people choose spouses of far different personality styles from their own. They marry because those differences bring variety, growth, and challenge as well as completeness to the relationship. They choose to accept those differences because of the enrichment variety adds to a relationship. Couples with any combination of personality styles are "capable of living together in harmony," which is *Webster's* definition of *compatibility*.

The second question is, Can opposites keep on attracting? By now you can guess that my answer to this is yes. Opposites can keep on attracting, but they must also keep on seeing differences as a positive part of the marriage relationship. If a person sees differences as a sign of incompatibility, or worse yet as a defect in the other person, then the marriage is headed for trouble.

The *reality* stage of marriage causes us to face our differences. It is the third stage of marriage, *recreation*, that helps us accept those differences and see them as assets rather than liabilities. *Recreation* literally means to create anew, restore to health, or refresh. The good news is that you can recreate your marriage relationship by learning to PLAY your marriage cards.

To help opposites keep on attracting and develop a winning hand in marriage, I suggest the PLAY strategies we used with children, with some basic differences.

Praise strengths
Laugh at differences
Accept personality
Yield

PRAISE STRENGTHS

A sure step to a winning hand in marriage is to start praising the strengths of your spouse, some of which you may perceive as weaknesses. For example, if you have an amiable spouse, you could say, "Andrea, I really appreciate your steadiness. I appreciate the fact that you're always there when I need you."

A relational wife could praise a conscientious husband by saying, "I'd like to tell you how much I appreciate the way you want things to look excellent around the house. I know I complain sometimes because I am so different, but your desire for quality adds to our family."

A conscientious spouse could praise her dominant partner by saying, "I appreciate how you want to make decisions and get work done. I know I drag my feet sometimes, but you bring good balance to our relationship."

You will be amazed at what happens to your relationship when you start praising the other person. Somehow the weakness seems to fade as we express appreciation for the uniqueness.

Turn to the marriage action plan (located on pages 175-176 near the end of this book). List two strengths in your spouse you will praise during the next week.

Laugh at Differences

You have to admit that the differences we have are sometimes hilarious. Let me tell you this story about Janet and myself. At about age fifty, I started making at least one bathroom adventure every night. Since many younger people have not experienced the thrill of negotiating a trip to the bathroom while three-quarters asleep, let me give you a blow-by-blow account.

The bladder pressure usually wakes me around about 2:00 a.m. I somehow manage to maneuver out of bed and get my feet on the floor. After the first two steps, I remember there is an ironing board obstacle that must be navigated around just past the end of the bed. If I make my first right turn in time, I will not hit it. Traveling on autopilot, I then make a left turn about five feet farther. If nothing has been left in the way, I arrive in the bathroom about ten feet later. A military left face, and I am ready for the greatest task of all—hitting the pot in the pitch dark. No problem for me. In fact, I even remember to put the toilet seat back down so my wife won't fall in on her trip.

I simply reverse the order of my voyage and return to my bed. But that's where the problem starts. My conscientious wife is such a perfectionist—such a neat freak—that she has made my side of the bed while I was gone. I get very confused: *My side of the bed is made*, I think. *Have I been to bed yet?* As the fog starts to lift, I determine that, since I have on my designer boxer shorts and my cute little T-shirt, I must have already been in bed. By this time I am wide awake and get back into bed and lie there thinking, *Why did I marry a conscientious wife?* Let me quickly add that the relational side of my personality persuaded me to embellish this story greatly! It is true that I do get up at night. It is also true that on some infrequent occasions my wife will straighten the covers and rearrange my pillow before my return trip is complete. It is also true that Janet and I have learned to enjoy our differences.

Just recently Janet and I were getting ready to leave for a trip. She brought out a map and said, "Would you like to look at this map before we leave?" Then she caught herself and quickly added, "What am I thinking of? Why should we break twenty-seven years of tradition by your looking at a map before we're half way to where we're going?" We both had a good laugh, and I did break tradition and looked at the map.

Janet and I have learned to laugh at our differences—not all the time, but often enough to remind ourselves not to take life too seriously. Studies of successful long-term married couples reveal that a sense of humor is one of the ingredients in marriages that last. Turn to the marriage action plan and write down two differences you can laugh at.

ACCEPT PERSONALITY

There is nothing more important to me than to be accepted by my wife. It is critical to our relationship for me to know that Janet doesn't think I have a defective personality. I do not mean, however, that Janet needs to understand or even like every part of my personality. I do need to know, however, that my dominant personality, with all its strengths and weaknesses, is accepted. Janet, likewise, needs to know I accept her conscientious personality. I may become irritated at certain aspects of her conscientious behavior, but I accept her personality because that is who she is.

When we constantly try to change our spouse—no matter how subtle that pressure might be—we are telling that person that he or she is unacceptable. Some of us went into marriage knowing there were some cards in our spouse's personality suit that we did not particularly like. "No sweat," we thought. "It will be a simple matter of helping my spouse discard those unwanted cards and draw some new and better cards—more like the cards in my suit."

This ill-fated notion does not die quickly. Some of us have a difficult time giving it up. Note this irrefutable fact: If we try to change our spouse, he or she will resist. It just doesn't work.

A better way is to accept our spouse, weaknesses and all. When people feel accepted, they're much more likely to make the changes they already know we want them to make. While we never change our personalities 180 degrees, we can modify certain behaviors to better meet the needs of our spouse.

Before going on, turn to the marriage action plan and complete the "Accept Personality" section.

Yield

Modifying our behavior is what yielding is all about. We are voluntarily adjusting a behavior in order to meet the needs of our spouse. When we do this, it is a sign that we esteem our spouse. It is a very practical application of the biblical admonition to "love one another." We don't lose our identity when we modify our behavior for a spouse. We simply adjust a certain behavior.

A specific example of this is how Janet yields to me in some areas. While she would really like me to be more of a perfectionist—especially around the house—she doesn't demand it. She adjusts her expectations and doesn't pressure me to live up to her standards. The ideal results are still there, but she chooses to accept less than those standards.

In a similar way, I yield voluntarily to her in the area of change. I change very quickly, but Janet takes much longer to make changes. I modify my behavior by not expecting her to change on my schedule. I give her time to get used to an idea, to research facts or whatever she needs to do. I try not to put her in positions where she will be pressured to change on my schedule and then feel resentful.

Turn to the marriage action plan and decide which personality trait in yourself you will modify for your spouse.

It is sometimes easier to accept one another and yield when we understand how our differences actually complete or complement one another in marriage. Following are listed four personality styles and how couples become a strong team because of the differences.

STYLE ────────▶	CONTRIBUTIONS ─▶	COMPLEMENTED ─▶ BY	COMPLETED BY
Conscientious	Cautious	Risk Takers	= Dominant and Relational
	Analytical	Visionaries	= Dominant and Relational
Amiable	Steady	Movers and Shakers	= Dominant and Relational
	Supportive	Decision Makers	= Dominant and Relational
Relational	Optimistic	Realists	= Conscientious and Amiable
	Spontaneous	Cautious	= Conscientious and Amiable
Dominant	Results Oriented	Quality Controllers	= Conscientious and Amiable
	Decisive	Researchers, Deliberaters	= Conscientious and Amiable

You can have a winning hand in marriage no matter how great your differences. As you have seen from this chapter, what matters in personality differences is how we perceive them. Decide now to PLAY a winning hand in your marriage. Good things are bound to happen.

Chapter Thirteen

Can Siblings Play Fairly?

Distressing outbursts such as "I can't stand Bobby" or "I hate Cindy" are among the worst words a parent can hear one child hurl at a brother or sister. We want our children to love, or at least not destroy, each other. We ask ourselves, "What can I do to help my children learn respect and tolerance for one another? How can I help them at least fight fairly when they're upset with one another?"

While there's no easy answer to helping brothers and sisters get along better, understanding personality styles can certainly help. One of the primary causes of sibling rivalry is the competition to be number one in the eyes of the parents. As a parent you are the prize, and each of your children would like to be your favorite. Thus each child competes to be "better" or more likable than the others. The more intense the competition, the more likely brothers and sisters will tear one another down to look more favorable in your eyes.

ARE YOU PLAYING FAIRLY?

All of us must ask ourselves the question, "Am I playing fairly?" It's not that we consciously fuel the fires of competition by favoring one child over another, but it can happen without our being aware of it. One primary way we do this is by valuing one personality style over another. This happens when we consistently praise some characteristic of one child's personality style while ignoring the uniqueness of another child.

The parents of the twin high school girls I mentioned earlier in the book are an example of valuing the personality of one child over another. One twin was like her parents, conscientious and amiable. The other twin was relational. The girl resembling her parents was made to feel good about herself, while the relational girl was made to feel that it was definitely not okay to be people oriented and impulsive. No wonder there was resentment and bitterness between these twins. These were not bad parents; they were good, loving parents who didn't understand differences in personalities.

Parents are not playing fairly when:

♦ They call attention to the "good" conscientious child while laughing about the "airhead" relational child.
♦ The dominant child is labeled "difficult" because of his aggressiveness, but the amiable child is labeled "good" because "she never gives us a bit of trouble."

HOW TO PLAY FAIRLY

Following are four ways to play fairly:

1. Celebrate your own uniqueness. In other words, find peace and joy that God has made you, in the words of the psalmist, "so wonderfully complex."[1]

2. Celebrate each child's uniqueness. The P in PLAY (Promote strengths) will help keep you on track in this area.
3. Practice unconditional love. Our children should never feel that they need to "qualify" for our love. Love based on achievement promotes sibling rivalry.
4. Don't compare. Remember, our children are already comparing themselves to one another. We should encourage our children only to live up to their God-given potential.

TEACHING YOUR CHILDREN TO PLAY FAIRLY

The goal of teaching our children to play fairly is to help them value their own uniqueness and the uniqueness of their brothers and sisters. The foundation, as we have seen, is our own example.

A second approach to teaching children to play fairly is to structure some family time for personality style education. Following are some ideas that can help the family learn together about the uniqueness of each individual. Choose the activities that best suit the ages and interests of your family.

Teaching Through Family Time Activities

Family Personality Style Assessment Time. Have a family time where the family works together to assess each person's personality style. Use the personality inventories in this book. After each family member has determined his or her personality style, have each person read aloud the thirteen characteristics of his or her suit. As the person reads have the rest of the family raise their hands if they have observed that characteristic in the person. (If children are of preschool age, you might just talk about the two or three major characteristics of your child's personality and not use the CARD terms.)

Personality Style Role Playing. A good way to under-stand another person's situation is to put yourself in that person's shoes. Role playing can give us a sense of what it's like to be a personality style other than our own. Plan a family time for family members to role play the personality style of another family member. This should be a fun learning experi-ence. Have family members act out as many other personality styles as they wish. Have a discussion afterward on how it felt to act out the other personalities. Discuss how it felt to see your personality being acted out by someone else.

What Would the World Be Like? Have a family discus-sion on what the world would be like if God had created every-one with the same personality style. Try, for example, to imag-ine how it would be if all the brain surgeons in the world were high relationals, or what would happen if every engineer was a high dominant. Discuss why God created people with different personalities.

Bible Personalities. Have a Bible discovery time with family members trying to find Bible personalities with the various personality styles. Clues: Moses was a conscientious; Abraham, an amiable; Peter, a relational; Joshua, a dominant; and Paul was probably a dominant/conscientious. Discover as many personality styles in the Bible as time allows. Discuss how God used these people and their uniqueness in special ways. Discuss how God will use each family member in special ways because of his or her uniqueness.

Who Am I? Have a family member secretly choose a per-sonality style and start reading, one at a time, the personality characteristics of that suit. The rest of the family then tries to guess the suit to which the characteristics belong. The first person to guess correctly selects the next suit and repeats the procedure.

My Ideal Day. Have each family member write on a sheet of paper what he or she would do on an "ideal day," assuming the person had unlimited resources and freedom. After everyone is done, read the summaries aloud. Have a discussion on the differences and similarities of each person's ideal day and how the distinctions reflect each person's uniqueness. Read and discuss Romans 15:7.

Circle of Appreciation. Give each person a sheet of paper with a circle on it, as shown in the following diagram. Each person is to enter his own name in the inner circle. He then passes his sheet to the person on his left, who writes in one section what he appreciates about the personality of that person and signs his name. He then passes it on to the next person who also writes what he appreciates about the person whose name is on the inner circle. This process continues until each person has written what he appreciates about each family member. The circles are returned to their owners. Each person, in turn, then reads aloud what the other members of the family appreciate about his personality.

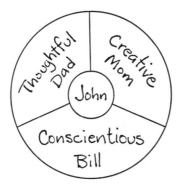

Teaching While It's Happening
A third way to teach brothers and sisters to play fairly with one another is during the heat of battle. It is also one of the most difficult times to teach because emotions often run so high.

Character Assassinations. Character assassinations usually have to do with name calling or derogatory remarks about the other person's intelligence or appearance. This can include such outright name calling as "You're stupid," or lower key statements like "You are so boring." In either case, the remarks are a kind of character assassination. The person feels attacked at the core of who he is and often will retaliate with an attack of his own.

When you observe this kind of interaction, it is time to step in and do some teaching. The child who is assaulting his brother's or sister's character is probably angry or hurt. You don't know what has preceded this encounter, so be careful not to assume that it is all the fault of the child carrying out the character assassination.

Stop the battle and give the warriors a few moments to cool down. Next, ask what happened. You will probably hear conflicting stories, with each child laying the blame on the other. Without taking sides, do these two things: First, reinforce the family rule that name calling will not be tolerated. I feel very strongly about this because I have seen the devastating effects of name calling over and over in the lives of people I counsel. The adage "Sticks and stones may break my bones, but words will never hurt me" is a lie! Words can pierce the soul and have lasting effects on self-esteem. Talk to the combatants about how much it hurts to be called names.

Next, explain that, while all people have conflict, it is important to fight fairly. Ask the children individually what they were really feeling. Help them identify their feelings of anger, hurt, fear, and so on. Encourage them to express feelings instead of attacking one another. Say such things as, "Brian, when you're angry with your brother, why don't you say, 'I get really angry when you take my things without asking,' instead of calling him 'scum.'" It's important to teach our children communication skills so they can *express* feelings appropriately instead of *acting* out feelings inappropriately.

Unfavorable Comparisons. Another teaching opportunity arises when we hear our children make unfavorable comparisons. Sometimes the comparison is unfavorable to the child making it. Your child might say, "Why does she always draw better than me?" This is a time for teaching about each child's uniqueness. You might say, "Jill, it's true that your sister has a gift for drawing, but let's talk about the gifts God has given you that your sister does not have."

At other times the comparisons are unfavorable to brothers or sisters. This usually means that the child is feeling "one down" or having some feelings of low self-esteem. I can remember both of our older daughters making unfavorable comparisons of each other. Heidi would say, "How can Liesl be so irresponsible?" In other words, compared to me (amiable/conscientious), Liesl (relational) does not measure up. Liesl, on the other hand, would talk about Heidi as being "boring" or "self-righteous." In both cases the girls were showing the other in an unfavorable light in an attempt to look better in our eyes and feel better about themselves.

When our children use these kinds of putdowns, it is an opportunity for us to once again reinforce their uniqueness and the uniqueness of the sibling they are comparing themselves to. We might say, "Yes, Heidi. I am aware that Liesl is often irresponsible in some areas, but she also adds to this family with her spontaneous and positive attitude. You tend to be more responsible and steady. You both add something special to this family because of your uniqueness."

RULES FOR PLAYING FAIRLY

I believe that every family should have some explicit, posted rules for playing fairly. I encourage you to make a list of rules that will diffuse sibling rivalry and help brothers and sisters honor one another's uniqueness. Parents can set a strong, positive example. Here are some ideas to get you started:

1. Honor one another's uniqueness (personality style, etc.).
2. Express feelings in a direct and loving way. (Say what you mean, mean what you say, and don't say it mean.)
3. No derogatory remarks about the other person's appearance.
4. No remarks about the other's intelligence.
5. No physical violence (hitting, grabbing, slapping, shoving, etc.).

There is nothing in this chapter that will ensure a peaceful home with no fighting. That will come in heaven. What the ideas in this chapter can do is help your children learn how to develop healthy relationships, beginning at home. These lessons will be learned slowly and never perfectly. Your effort will be rewarded with *improved* relationships.

Chapter Fourteen

A Winning Hand at School

The consequence of a teacher not understanding personality styles could have a disastrous effect on your child. It did on one of ours.

In 1979 we moved to Napa, California. Bridget was going into the fourth grade at the time, so we enrolled her in a nearby elementary school. Little did we know the kind of year she was going to have.

Bridget seemed very unhappy those first few months, but we thought it was just because she was adjusting to a new school, new friends, and so on.

When Janet went to the first parent conference we were both disturbed by what was said. "Bridget's teacher says she's not getting along very well," Janet reported. "She says Bridget is not concentrating, is hyper, and is disturbing the rest of the class. But something else the teacher said really bothered me. She said I surprised her. She thought that Bridget's mother was going to be 'flighty' like Bridget."

We were concerned about the teacher's attitude toward Bridget. She had already decided that Bridget was an irresponsible airhead. In her estimation, Bridget was headed for a "life of failure" (her actual words).

We also believed Bridget had a responsibility to cope and improve her behavior. We realized she could be hyperactive and needed to be more disciplined in the classroom.

As the year went on, Bridget became more and more unhappy, both at school and at home. She seemed angry much of the time. She reported, "None of the kids like me." The reports from the teacher were all the same: "Bridget's in trouble."

We became so concerned that we asked for a school psychologist to start working with Bridget and us. Nothing seemed to help. Toward the end of the year we did what I thought we would never do: We asked to have Bridget moved to another class. This went against our basic belief that you do not bail children out, because there is growth through struggle. Our decision was based on the belief that Bridget's self-esteem was being damaged.

Contributing to the problem was the fact that Bridget's teacher was struggling in her classroom. She was a conscientious teacher under extreme pressure in her personal life, trying to cope with a nervous, insecure relational child who was trying to adjust to a new school. This is a classic example of a teacher and child with opposite personalities struggling to get along. The conscientious teacher was perfectionistic, reserved, and detailed, with a high need for control and structure. Bridget, with her relational personality, was talkative, disorganized, people oriented, change oriented, and emotional. The stage was set for conflict.

The teacher played only with the cards that came from suits to which she could relate. The relational suit was certainly not one of them. She had decided that a relational child was bad, irresponsible, heading for a life of failure, and almost certainly being reared by a mother with the same "problems."

At this point you are probably saying, "What a horrible teacher. Didn't she care?" She was not a horrible teacher, and she did care. I am convinced she really wanted to do what was right but just did not understand differences in personalities. She did very well with the children whose personalities didn't conflict with hers.

I have cited this example not to bad-mouth the teacher or the school. Both were trying to do their best in the complex task of teaching. Their best was not good enough in this case, however, because their knowledge was incomplete. With most children there will not be the disastrous results that Bridget experienced. It was years before she recouped from the disaster of the fourth grade. I am pleased to report that she has made the grade and is a delightful, well-adjusted high school graduate who works as a lead teacher at a preschool. Her plans include college, which refutes the gloomy predictions of her teacher.

Many children are resilient and can overcome the problems that surface from having personality differences with their teachers. This chapter, however, is to help you prevent the kind of trauma that Bridget experienced from happening to your child. Most cases will not be as severe as Bridget's. In less severe situations parents will be able to explain to their child why he may get along with one teacher better than another, or why a teacher seems to have problems relating to him.

I am not saying it's the total responsibility of the teacher to adjust to the child, or that you should expect this. It is also the child's responsibility to adjust to the teacher's personality. I hope you will be able to take what you have learned in this book about personality styles and teach it to your children.

Their ability to adjust to others will be invaluable.

The following material on student and teacher personality styles has two purposes. First, it will help you better understand your child's behavioral tendencies in the classroom and the kind of environment he needs to succeed. Second, it will help you understand how the personality style of the teacher is likely to affect the way he responds to your child. This information will give you the tools to help both your child and possibly the teacher adjust to one another within the classroom.

THE CHILD'S PERSONALITY STYLE IN THE CLASSROOM

The Conscientious Student

Conscientious students will want to be accurate and will hate making mistakes. Doing thorough, excellent work is important to conscientious students, so they will tend to get depressed, frustrated, or down on themselves when they're not living up to their own standards. Since these students tend to define themselves by what they do, not doing well is devastating.

Conscientious children like to see the big picture. They want to know why they are doing something. Since they are highly analytical, they are frustrated by assignments that don't make sense to them.

These students also don't like change. They want a predictable classroom atmosphere that gives adequate time to complete assignments thoroughly. They're the most private of the four styles and don't like teachers to single them out for attention. They generally have a few close friends and prefer working alone.

Conscientious students will be most frustrated by the faster-paced, change-oriented dominant and relational teachers. They generally respond better to the slower paced, more detail- and quality-oriented amiable and conscientious teachers.

The Amiable Student

Amiable students are often looked at as the "good" children by teachers. These children enjoy helping the teacher and usually have congenial relationships with the other students. They enjoy teachers who take time to be friendly with them and show appreciation for their efforts to help.

Amiable students enjoy a teacher who provides a predictable environment within the classroom—no sudden change. They are frustrated by highly unstructured classrooms and need to know exactly what is expected and the steps they can follow to complete the task.

Amiable students work well in a group but will seldom take charge. They will work hard to keep peace in the classroom and rarely show their inner feelings.

Amiable students can be frustrated by a high energy, change-oriented dominant or relational teacher. While not appreciating the unpredictability of the relational teacher, they will enjoy the teacher's warm, outgoing personality. Amiable children usually respond best to the slower-paced, more predictable amiable and conscientious teachers.

The Relational Student

Relational students are usually the most spontaneous and emotional in the class—and also the most talkative. For these students the best things about school are the relationships. They thrive on social approval. Because of this, their greatest fear is loss of social approval.

Relational students dislike details and paperwork and will often forget the teacher's instructions or lose their assignments. They like a positive, exciting classroom with maximum change and are especially bored with factual lectures that contain detail and omit stories about people.

Relational students generally love having a relational teacher in the classroom. They often become good friends because both have a high people orientation and expressiveness.

The relational student also will have good relationships with the dominant teacher because this teacher type also likes change, is not concerned with detail, and is fast paced.

The relational child will have the most difficulty relating to the conscientious teacher because of that teacher's methodical, structured, detail-oriented approach to managing the classroom. The relational student also will have some frustration with the amiable teacher's slow pace and desire for a predictable environment.

The Dominant Student

Dominant students are the most impatient of the four styles and are mostly interested in getting the work done—and often, not too well done. Finishing is their major goal. If a teacher's instructions are long or detailed, he will lose the dominant child.

Dominant children feel a need to be in charge. They like to have a high level of control and influence over a group. They can be motivated by a significant challenge, problem to solve, or other type of leadership responsibility.

Because of their dominance and occasional low people orientation, dominant students can be perceived as "pushy" and resented by other students. Since they want quick results, they often need help in seeing the importance of quality work.

A dominant student usually has the most trouble relating to a conscientious teacher. The conscientious teacher's attention to detail and desire for quality put him at odds with the dominant child. The dominant student also will have some frustration with an amiable teacher because of the slower pace and low-key approach. The student will have the easiest time in the classroom of a dominant or relational teacher. The faster pace and less structured approach of these teachers are better suited to the needs of the dominant child.

TEACHER PERSONALITY STYLES
IN THE CLASSROOM

The Conscientious Teacher

The conscientious teacher needs structure in the classroom. The day is organized so things go as planned. There are very few surprises. The room is usually neat and orderly.

This teacher type wants the students to complete their assignments according to his expectations. It is important to the teacher that students follow instructions to the letter. This teacher needs to maintain control of the class, which is done through organization and expectations, both for the children's behavior and classroom tasks.

The teacher usually responds well to conscientious and amiable students. These students fit well into the conscientious teacher's goals of a highly structured and controlled classroom. The conscientious teacher has a more difficult time understanding the more assertive and change-oriented relational and dominant students. The conscientious teacher sometimes sees dominant students as troublemakers because of their dominance and as unmotivated because they get bored easily and strive for quantity instead of quality.

The conscientious teacher also may have problems with a relational student within the classroom. The relational's expressiveness can be seen as "airheadedness" and the lack of organization as "irresponsibility."

The Amiable Teacher

The amiable teacher wants routine in the classroom but needs less structure than the conscientious teacher does. Things are generally done in a predictable manner with little change in routine.

This teacher is interested not only in the product but also in the personal relationships within the classroom. He wants peace and harmony among students and himself, is generally interested in the welfare of the students, and works at having congenial relationships with both students and teachers.

The amiable teacher is most often a "helper" in the classroom, supporting or directing the efforts of the children in a low-key way.

Generally, amiable and conscientious children respond best to the classroom environment of an amiable teacher. They like the routine and predictability.

The amiable teacher is often well liked by all the students, but relational and dominant students may complain that the class is a little boring. They would like more change and excitement. The teacher may react internally to fast-paced dominant and relational children who sometimes challenge the limits of control and press for more creativity and flexibility. But this teacher will be more accepting and supportive of differences than the more perfectionistic conscientious teacher.

The Relational Teacher

The relational teacher likes change and excitement in the classroom. His classroom often reflects this by bright colors and fun things to do. The relational teacher likes to do spontaneous things in the classroom and sometimes is disorganized. He teaches with great enthusiasm.

This teacher desires a warm friendly relationship with the students and also wants students to get along well with one another.

The relational teacher usually loves relational students. Because of their mutual expressiveness, relational teachers and students see each other as exciting and fun to be with. The relational teacher usually relates better to the dominant child than does the amiable or conscientious teacher, but all teachers are bothered some by the dominant child's low people orientation with other students.

The relational teacher can be frustrated by the conscientious student's questions and desire to know exactly what is required. The relational teacher sometimes will want conscientious children to "come out of their shell" and be more outgoing.

Like all teachers, the relational teacher likes the amiable child. He is often not aware of the amiable child's need for less change and more structure in the classroom. The amiable child usually wants to please the teacher too much to let him know about his frustration.

The Dominant Teacher

The dominant teacher likes to control the classroom and usually does so with force of character. There is never a question of who is in charge of the dominant teacher's classroom.

This teacher teaches for results. The bottom line is what is important. He wants the students to "just do the work" and not ask questions about details that he sees as unimportant. The dominant teacher's instructions are often "bare bones"—succinct and to the point.

The dominant teacher can be impatient with the student who needs a lot of time and attention. Since the teacher doesn't have a high people orientation, he is sometimes looked at by students and parents as uncaring or unfriendly.

This teacher usually relates well to a dominant student because of their similar characteristics. If the dominant student, however, challenges for control, that is another story!

The dominant teacher is sometimes irritated by the slow pace of the amiable student. The conscientious student, however, is the most difficult for the dominant teacher to relate to. He cannot understand the student's resistance to change and desire to know every detail of an assignment. The conscientious child's "why" questions will drive the dominant teacher crazy.

WHAT CAN A PARENT DO?

By now you are probably thinking, "But what can I do about my child's school? I don't have control over the teachers." While it is true that you cannot force a school or teacher to play a winning hand, there are some things you can do.

First, you can teach your children about personality styles. Children in the lower grades won't understand, but older children will. Understanding personality styles can help your children in two ways. They will be able to see that conflict with a teacher can result from personality differences and not because there is something wrong with the child—or the teacher. The child will come to see himself as different from the teacher, not defective. You can also teach your children that they are responsible to modify their behavior to better adapt to the needs of the teacher. I realize this is asking a lot of children, but as they mature they can learn this valuable skill. You'll need to emphasize that you are not asking them to change *who they are*, but to modify, temporarily, some behavior because of the current situation. This training will help them to improve relationships for the rest of their lives.

There is a second thing you can do. You can talk to your child's teacher about personality styles. Teachers may or may not be open to this kind of input. They may think you're making excuses for your child's behavior or lack of achievement. They could become defensive, thinking you are criticizing them. Some teachers, however, will want to hear what you have to say. Give them a copy of this book and let them read this chapter. Have a follow-up discussion on how personality differences are affecting your child's performance in the classroom.

Many good teachers adapt their teaching styles to the needs of the students without a knowledge of personality styles. Most teachers, however, could use additional training in this area.

◆

Chapter Fifteen

The Winning Parent

You are a winner! How do I know? Because you cared enough about your family relationships to purchase this book and hang on until the final chapter! Winners are always looking for ways to improve. They are open to new ideas and willing to move from their comfort zones into unexplored frontiers.

There is another characteristic I have noticed about people who succeed: They look at the past to learn valuable lessons, but they will not dwell on past imperfections. Their thinking goes like this, "Sure, I have made some mistakes as a parent, admittedly I have not played my cards as well as I could have in the past. But now that I understand personality styles, I will put that information to work. *I can and will improve my relationships!*"

While winners are always looking for ways to strengthen family relationships, they don't expect them to be perfect. Setting standards too high can cause us to feel like losers. *If you take half of what you have learned in this book and use it half of the time, you will see pleasing results.*

Winners have faith—in God and in themselves. A winner's belief system says, "I can do everything God asks me to with the help of Christ who gives me the strength and power."[1] Winners know they can do their part to improve family relationships because of the inner strength supplied through Christ.

Finally, a winner always knows he has hope and a future because of God's love. The Bible is full of promises to His people, like this one: "For I know the plans I have for you, says the Lord. They are plans for good and not for evil, to give you a future and a hope."[2]

God has good plans for you in your family relationships. You are a winner through Him! May God continue to bless you and your family.

PARENTING ACTION PLAN

Child's Name _____ Child's Personality Style _____

PROMOTE STRENGTHS

Two strengths: 1. _____ 2. _____

I will promote these strengths by:

1. _____

2. _____

LIMIT WEAKNESSES

Two weaknesses: 1. _____ 2. _____

I will limit these weaknesses by:

1. _____

2. _____

ACCEPT PERSONALITY

I will accept my child's personality by changing my attitudes and actions in

these ways: _____

_____

YOUR COMPATIBILITY

My natural compatibility with my child is _____
(poor, fair, good, excellent).

My own personality characteristic that is most difficult for my child to

cope with is _____

In order to create a better environment for my child, I will adjust that

characteristic in the following way: _____

_____

PARENTING ACTION PLAN

Child's Name _____ Child's Personality Style _____

PROMOTE STRENGTHS

Two strengths: 1. _____ 2. _____

I will promote these strengths by:

1. _____

2. _____

LIMIT WEAKNESSES

Two weaknesses: 1. _____ 2. _____

I will limit these weaknesses by:

1. _____

2. _____

ACCEPT PERSONALITY

I will accept my child's personality by changing my attitudes and actions in

these ways: _____

_____

YOUR COMPATIBILITY

My natural compatibility with my child is _____
(poor, fair, good, excellent).

My own personality characteristic that is most difficult for my child to

cope with is _____

In order to create a better environment for my child, I will adjust that

characteristic in the following way: _____

_____

PARENTING ACTION PLAN

Child's Name _____ Child's Personality Style _____

PROMOTE STRENGTHS

Two strengths: 1. _____ 2. _____

I will promote these strengths by:

1. _____

2. _____

LIMIT WEAKNESSES

Two weaknesses: 1. _____ 2. _____

I will limit these weaknesses by:

1. _____

2. _____

ACCEPT PERSONALITY

I will accept my child's personality by changing my attitudes and actions in

these ways: _____

_____

YOUR COMPATIBILITY

My natural compatibility with my child is _____
(poor, fair, good, excellent).

My own personality characteristic that is most difficult for my child to

cope with is _____

In order to create a better environment for my child, I will adjust that

characteristic in the following way: _____

_____

PARENTING ACTION PLAN

Child's Name _____ Child's Personality Style _____

PROMOTE STRENGTHS

Two strengths: 1. _____ 2. _____

I will promote these strengths by:

1. _____

2. _____

LIMIT WEAKNESSES

Two weaknesses: 1. _____ 2. _____

I will limit these weaknesses by:

1. _____

2. _____

ACCEPT PERSONALITY

I will accept my child's personality by changing my attitudes and actions in
these ways: _____

_____

YOUR COMPATIBILITY

My natural compatibility with my child is _____
(poor, fair, good, excellent).

My own personality characteristic that is most difficult for my child to
cope with is _____

In order to create a better environment for my child, I will adjust that
characteristic in the following way: _____

_____

PARENTING ACTION PLAN

Child's Name _____ Child's Personality Style _____

PROMOTE STRENGTHS

Two strengths: 1. _____ 2. _____

I will promote these strengths by:

1. _____

2. _____

LIMIT WEAKNESSES

Two weaknesses: 1. _____ 2. _____

I will limit these weaknesses by:

1. _____

2. _____

ACCEPT PERSONALITY

I will accept my child's personality by changing my attitudes and actions in these ways: _____

_____

YOUR COMPATIBILITY

My natural compatibility with my child is _____
(poor, fair, good, excellent).

My own personality characteristic that is most difficult for my child to cope with is _____

In order to create a better environment for my child, I will adjust that characteristic in the following way: _____

_____

PARENTING ACTION PLAN

Child's Name _____ Child's Personality Style _____

PROMOTE STRENGTHS

Two strengths: 1. _____ 2. _____

I will promote these strengths by:

1. _____

2. _____

LIMIT WEAKNESSES

Two weaknesses: 1. _____ 2. _____

I will limit these weaknesses by:

1. _____

2. _____

ACCEPT PERSONALITY

I will accept my child's personality by changing my attitudes and actions in these ways: _____

_____

YOUR COMPATIBILITY

My natural compatibility with my child is _____
(poor, fair, good, excellent).

My own personality characteristic that is most difficult for my child to cope with is _____

In order to create a better environment for my child, I will adjust that characteristic in the following way: _____

_____

PARENTING ACTION PLAN

Child's Name _____ Child's Personality Style _____

PROMOTE STRENGTHS

Two strengths: 1. _____ 2. _____

I will promote these strengths by:

1. _____

2. _____

LIMIT WEAKNESSES

Two weaknesses: 1. _____ 2. _____

I will limit these weaknesses by:

1. _____

2. _____

ACCEPT PERSONALITY

I will accept my child's personality by changing my attitudes and actions in

these ways: _____

_____

YOUR COMPATIBILITY

My natural compatibility with my child is _____
(poor, fair, good, excellent).

My own personality characteristic that is most difficult for my child to

cope with is _____

In order to create a better environment for my child, I will adjust that

characteristic in the following way: _____

_____

PARENTING ACTION PLAN

Child's Name _____ Child's Personality Style _____

PROMOTE STRENGTHS

Two strengths: 1. _____ 2. _____

I will promote these strengths by:

1. _____

2. _____

LIMIT WEAKNESSES

Two weaknesses: 1. _____ 2. _____

I will limit these weaknesses by:

1. _____

2. _____

ACCEPT PERSONALITY

I will accept my child's personality by changing my attitudes and actions in
these ways: _____

_____

YOUR COMPATIBILITY

My natural compatibility with my child is _____
(poor, fair, good, excellent).

My own personality characteristic that is most difficult for my child to
cope with is _____

In order to create a better environment for my child, I will adjust that
characteristic in the following way: _____

_____

MARRIAGE ACTION PLAN

Spouse's name_____ Spouse's Personality Style _____

PRAISE STRENGTHS

Two strengths: 1. _____ 2. _____

I will praise these strengths by:

1. _____

2. _____

LAUGH AT DIFFERENCES

Two differences: 1. _____ 2. _____

I will laugh at these differences by:

1. _____

2. _____

ACCEPT PERSONALITY

I will accept my spouse's personality by changing my attitudes and actions

in these ways: _____

_____

YIELD

My personality trait that is most difficult for my spouse to cope with is:

_____

I will yield by modifying that trait in the following way: _____

_____

(You may want to ask your spouse to suggest a trait for you to modify.)

MARRIAGE ACTION PLAN

Spouse's name_____ Spouse's Personality Style _____

PRAISE STRENGTHS

Two strengths: 1. _____ 2. _____

I will praise these strengths by:

1. _____

2. _____

LAUGH AT DIFFERENCES

Two differences: 1. _____ 2. _____

I will laugh at these differences by:

1. _____

2. _____

ACCEPT PERSONALITY

I will accept my spouse's personality by changing my attitudes and actions
in these ways: _____

_____

YIELD

My personality trait that is most difficult for my spouse to cope with is:

_____

I will yield by modifying that trait in the following way: _____

_____

(You may want to ask your spouse to suggest a trait for you to modify.)

Notes

INTRODUCTION

1. Performax is a division of Carlson Learning Companies, 12755 State Highway 55, Minneapolis. MN 55441. Carlson Learning Companies distributes three excellent resources to help people determine their personality style. First is their standard Personal Profile System; second is their Biblical Profile System (this is similar to the Personal Profile System except it integrates biblical material into the profiles). The third resource is their Child's Profile that uses a cartoon character instead of words to help determine the child's personality style. For more information on these tools, contact Carlson Learning Companies.
2. David W. Merill and Roger H. Reid, *Personal Styles and Effective Performance: Making Your Style Work for You* (Radnor, PA: Chilton Book Co., 1981).
3. John 13:34.

CHAPTER ONE—DID SOMEONE STACK THE DECK?

1. Psalm 139:13-14.
2. Romans 15:7, NIV.
3. Romans 12:10.

CHAPTER SEVEN—DEVELOPING A WINNING HAND

1. 1 John 3:18, italics in original.
2. Proverbs 22:6.
3. Romans 15:7, NIV.

CHAPTER THIRTEEN—CAN SIBLINGS PLAY FAIRLY?

1. Psalm 139:14.

CHAPTER FIFTEEN—THE WINNING PARENT

1. Philippians 4:13.
2. Jeremiah 29:11.